THE POLITICS OF
REPRESENTATION

POLITICAL COMMUNICATION

FRONTIERS IN

Lynda Lee Kaid and Bruce Gronbeck
General Editors

Vol. 5

PETER LANG
New York • Washington, D.C./Baltimore • Bern
Frankfurt am Main • Berlin • Brussels • Vienna • Oxford

Juliet Roper, Christina Holtz-Bacha,
Gianpietro Mazzoleni

★ ★ ★

THE POLITICS OF REPRESENTATION

Election Campaigning and
Proportional Representation

★ ★ ★

PETER LANG
New York • Washington, D.C./Baltimore • Bern
Frankfurt am Main • Berlin • Brussels • Vienna • Oxford

Library of Congress Cataloging-in-Publication Data

Roper, Juliet.
The politics of representation: election campaigning and
proportional representation / Juliet Roper, Christina Holtz-Bacha,
Gianpietro Mazzoleni, plus a chapter by Douglas Kellner.
p. cm. — (Frontiers in political communication; vol. 5)
Includes bibliographical references and index.
1. Proportional representation. 2. Democracy. 3. Political campaigns.
I. Holtz-Bacha, Christina. II. Mazzoleni, Gianpietro.
III. Title. IV. Frontiers in political communication; v. 5.
JF1071.R66 324.7—dc21 2002067547
ISBN 0-8204-6148-2
ISSN 1525-9730

Bibliographic information published by **Die Deutsche Bibliothek**.
Die Deutsche Bibliothek lists this publication in the "Deutsche
Nationalbibliografie"; detailed bibliographic data is available
on the Internet at http://dnb.ddb.de/.

Cover design by Joni Holst

The paper in this book meets the guidelines for permanence and durability
of the Committee on Production Guidelines for Book Longevity
of the Council of Library Resources.

© 2004 Peter Lang Publishing, Inc., New York
275 Seventh Avenue, 28th Floor, New York, NY 10001
www.peterlangusa.com

Printed in the United States of America

Table of Contents

Part One

Introduction: Proportional Representation and Democracy

While many may regard the ancient Athenian model of direct democracy as an ideal, in spite of the fact that the franchise excluded the majority of Greek adults, it is generally agreed that a process that involves all citizens in legislative decision making is both impractical and, arguably, undesirable in large modern societies. Although the advent of technology to facilitate the instant aggregation of responses to referenda from widely dispersed communities may have revitalised the possibilities for direct democracy on an issue–by–issue basis, it is unlikely that voters would want to, or would be able to, allocate the time necessary for such participation. A further requirement would be the provision of full and balanced information in order for voters to form a rational opinion. What is the potential for such a provision? Could private interests be put aside in the interests of ascertaining the collective good? These are the democratic ideals that form the essence of the Habermasian public sphere (Habermas, 1991). They are, however, rarely the reality as, for many and diverse reasons, modern democracies fall short of the ideal.

Modern liberal democracies are based upon the principles of representative democracy. Indeed, the institution of elections is today one of the central tenets of democracy for it is through elections that citizens choose those who will represent them in the formation of public policy and in the governing of their country. The principle of representation is, however, problematic, and needs to be considered from a range of perspectives, including the degree to which diverse interests are actually given voice in legislative assemblies. To a large extent this will be dependent upon the nature of the electoral system.

Representation can usefully be examined as a two–way process. On the one hand, individuals (citizens) in civil society seek representation of their interests in the formation of public policy. On the other hand, those who seek (re)election represent themselves to voters through the creation of an identity (often at least partially in the form of a manifesto), which is designed to articulate (Hall, 1986; Slack, 1996) or connect the interests of the represented with those of the representative. In modern society neither representation of civil society nor representation to voters by politicians can be achieved without the intervention of the mass media. Indeed, as Dahlgren (1995) points out "just as representation in democracy is unavoidable, so is representation in communication" (p. 16). It is through the media that the two sides of political representation meet, giving the media considerable responsibility for the functioning of a public sphere. The degree to which the media fulfill that responsibility depends upon national variables, including the regulatory framework within which the media operate.

The most common institution for the representation of candidates to citizens is that of election campaigns. This book examines systems of proportional representation from each side of the dual process of representation and from the perspectives of three culturally and historically different countries: Germany, New Zealand, and Italy. Part One details the development and the democratic potential of each country's particular configuration of electoral system for representation of diverse and conflicting interests. Part Two compares the election campaign practices of each of these three countries with dominant campaign theory, which has emerged primarily from two countries with plurality electoral systems, Britain and the United States. Part Three takes the 2000 USA presidential campaign as a case study of an election held under a majoritarian system in a chapter contributed by Douglas Kellner. As explored in the introduction to Part Two, current models of election campaigning are often attributed to those developed in the USA, with a dominant influence of the mass media both in campaign development and in the role of dissemination of information to voters. Thus, Part Three, through its examination of the extraordinary culmination of campaign strategies of the 2000 USA election, provides a basis for examination of the ways in which national differences in culture, history, and electoral system impact upon election campaigns.

Representation of citizens

It is to the political field that citizens elect their representatives in order that they may act on citizens' behalf. The degree to which citizens can be represented, however, is subject to numerous variables, including the degree (in practice) of alignment between elected representatives and those whom they purport to represent. The electoral system clearly has a direct effect upon the range of interests that can be represented in legislative assemblies. Plurality, or first–past–the–post systems, in principle, awards legislative power to the party that receives the majority (or plurality) of votes. Elections under such systems are run simultaneously within a number of geographically defined districts or constituencies in order to select constituency representatives. The party with the majority of elected representatives is awarded overall power in the national assembly. Britain's Westminster system is the most well–known plurality electoral system. Plurality systems can, however, and very often do, produce disproportional election results (Lijphart, 1999). Because governmental power is decided upon an aggregate of constituency results on a first–past–the–post basis, the winner is not necessarily the party or the candidate with the overall majority of the vote. Thus, the key interests of a majority of voters may not be represented directly in government. This is particularly so in those countries whose governments have a powerful, single party cabinet (Lijphart).

Even under systems of proportional representation the practicalities of a close alignment of the wide range of citizens' interests and a relatively small number of elected representatives present substantial difficulties. Nation–states are, with few exceptions, formed with geographical and legislative boundaries, rather than through homogeneous groupings of citizens. On the contrary, most nations are made up of numerous diverse groups that could be loosely categorised according to sociological, cultural, or institutional factors (Birch, 1993). Political represen–tation of diverse groups is rendered even more complex by the fact that individuals can identify themselves simultaneously with each of a range of such groups. The range of subject positions thus occupied by individual voters can cause the individual to shift between multiple and often contradictory concerns (Moffitt, 1994).

The political field, according to Bourdieu (1991), is bounded by poles that constitute the limits of what is politically thinkable, or acceptable, at a given time and place. That is, there will be some interests and opinions held by small minorities that will be marginalized outside the current political field and, therefore will not be represented in legislative debate. In Western democracies political fields are most commonly polarized ideologically by expressions of Left and Right (Lijphart, 1999). Polarization, however, is not always evident. Where there is policy consensus amongst the majority of political representatives, those policies can be neutralized in the center of the political field (Bourdieu, 1991). Neutralization increases as representatives seek to maximize their support base by articulating their policies with what is perceived to be the majority of public opinion, resulting in a tendency for aggregation in the political center. Such a merging of political opponents in a central position is considered more likely to occur when a country is in a period of political stability, free from political turmoil. Political parties that merge in a central position in order to maximize their role as representative of multiple interests in a socially diverse civil society are known as "catch–all" parties (Kirchheimer, 1966). As other parties also seek to maximize the range of voters' interests they represent, differentiation between the parties becomes difficult, especially on ideological grounds as Left/Right positioning becomes blurred.

A lack of a clear differentiation between political opponents raises concerns for the democratic process. One of the principle concerns is that citizens fail to participate in politics, thus effectively removing themselves from the public sphere. As Mouffe (1993) states:

> liberal democracy [or other forms of radical democracy] calls for the constitution of collective identities around clearly differentiated positions and the possibility of choosing real alternatives . . . [A lack of binary (or multiple) opposition] means that the current blurring of political frontiers between Left and Right is harmful for democratic politics, as it impedes the constitution of distinctive political identities. This in turn fosters disaffection towards political parties and discourages participation in the political process (p. 5).

Participation in the political process is one of the key factors in the viability of a public sphere, yet the United States where catch–all parties dominate, records one of the lowest rates of voter participation of any democratic country in the world (Gans, 1988; Reilly, 1996).

From another perspective, Birch (1993, p. 84) suggests that ideological differentiation between political parties is a contributing factor to a higher level of public interest in political issues. His perspective has much more recently been corroborated by van Kempen (2002) in a study of the European elections of 1999. Polarization of political parties, however, or a lack of it, is not the only factor that encourages or discourages voter participation in elections. Even though political parties may seek to occupy the center ground, sometimes deliberately avoiding polarization by avoiding to take a clear stance on certain issues or by avoiding those issues altogether, a partisan media can also generate polarization amongst voters by openly favoring one political party or candidate over another. The tendency for the media to take such a role varies from nation to nation. Whereas in some countries, such as New Zealand, the media claim political impartiality; others, such as Britain, have a strongly partisan press. Italy (see Chapter Six) has seen the use of private media to bolster support for the owner of the media, Berlusconi, in his successful bids for electoral victory.

In an effort to maintain differentiation within a political field characterized by a strong, neutral center and relatively weak poles, the parties of the center are likely to turn to personal attributes. Characteristics such as "honesty" or "integrity" cannot be contested within the political field as issues on an ideological basis. That is, they cannot be drawn into arguments of Left versus Right. If they cannot be thus contested, they cannot be neutralized in a political center. As Mouffe (1993) maintains, a divergence of political positions and interests "can too easily be replaced by a confrontation between non–negotiable moral values and essentialist identities" (p. 6).

The strength of the poles of a political field as well as the relative dominance of a particular ideology will determine the degree to which political parties can occupy the neutral center of the field. In times of social upheaval, demands made upon the political field by social groups are increased. Under such circumstances, political parties cannot easily neutralize ideologically based issues through establishing one perspective as common sense because of the increased support for opposing views. While it may be contended that catch–all parties are becoming less viable in an increasingly heterogeneous society (Haeusler and Hirsch, 1989), they are still a strong feature of Western democracies. Their continued viability is dependent upon "the existence of a stable 'hegemonial structure' that in turn is based on the compatibility of social experiences and political forms of interest regulation" (p. 311). It is also dependent upon an electoral system that marginalizes the voices of smaller, more narrowly focused political parties.

The number of political parties that occupy a political field with a position of influence in government is another factor that is likely to affect the potential for parties to merge ideologically in the neutral center. To a large extent this will be determined by the electoral system that governs the dynamics of the political field. Under a plurality system such as first–past–the–post, one political party is likely to form a government. Coalition governments are unlikely and dissenting voices can more easily be marginalized outside the sphere of policy formation. Under a system of proportional representation, however, minor parties can have direct influence in government. This means that a greater range of social representation is possible with a correspondingly greater range of voices heard within the political field. Although under systems of proportional representation political parties can still seek to occupy the political center, there is still scope for parties to represent important issues that might otherwise be ignored. This has been the case in New Zealand where the Green Party in the 2002 election took a strong stance against the introduction of field trials of genetically modified organisms in the country (see Chapter Five). In Germany the two big parties both claim the center ground for themselves but, again in 2002, it was the minor parties that influenced the outcome of the election by taking a clear stance on particular issues. Minor parties' influence is relatively strong because they can determine the direction of power by supporting a major party in coalition.

There is a further issue regarding the representation of interests within the political field and that is the ability of certain powerful elites within society to secure political representation more readily and with greater effect than others. The question raised earlier of whether or not private interests could, or would, be put aside in favor of a "public good" is an important one. While social groups of civil society can use numbers to influence policy formation in accordance with a majority public will, policy formation is also influenced from the economic sphere embodied in corporations and other business interests. Such groups have a clear private interest in public policy exerting influence upon policy formation to the extent that the boundaries between governments and corporations can become blurred (Nadel, 1976). Mutual dependency between governments and corporations can also develop, depending on the regulations applied within individual nation–states, through the provision of financial support for the election campaigns of candidates who are perceived to be sympathetic to the donors' interests. This inevitably raises the question of legitimacy: How can governments represent the interests of civil society against the interests of those who, in effect, paid to have the government elected? In plurality electoral systems, the potential for corporate influence in public policy formation is arguably greater as lobbyists (through campaign donations or through other means of attempted influence) need only negotiate with a very small number of potential policy makers. Under systems of proportional representation lobbyists must negotiate not only with a greater number of policy makers but also with a wider range of interest representatives. Thus, influence becomes potentially more complicated and difficult. The same arguments apply to influence from other non–governmental interest groups, such as environmental groups or single issue groups such as the powerful American National Rifle Association (NRA).

Under electoral systems of proportional representation, then, it can be argued that there is greater potential for representation of the diverse interests of civil society within political fields. The parallel argument can also be made that proportional represen–tation does not work in the narrow interests of dominant political parties or sectional interests that seek to pursue their own agenda. Any changes in the electoral system would, therefore, be likely to be subject to intense conflict as opposing groups sought to maximize their particular sphere of influence. The ways in which these differences may or may not be manifest will depend upon cultural, social, and historical variables.

Regardless of the electoral system, political candidates that seek to represent civil society in the political sphere must successfully represent themselves to civil society. Such is the duality of representation that is the focus of this book. Those who are in office must continually represent themselves as working in the interests of voters and, at election times, all candidates must (re)present themselves as desirable leaders of the country. The election campaigns that ensue and the messages that they disseminate have to be planned with national differences taken into account. Thus, the two sides of the duality are interdependent.

Chapter One

Germany: The "German Model" and Its Intricacies

The most important step toward re-democratization in Germany after the Second World War and toward regaining sovereignty was the promulgation in May 1949 of the *Basic Law*, the new constitution of the Federal Republic of Germany. While the occupying powers gradually retreated and left the political power more and more to the Germans, the forming of the new state also sealed the separation of the three Western occupation zones (American, British, French) from the Eastern zone, occupied by the Soviets, finally leading to a divided country. Under Soviet influence and integrated into the East European economic and military organizations, East Germany took a socialist turn and developed into an authoritarian state, the German Democratic Republic (GDR). The Federal Republic of Germany (FRG) on the other side, pursuing a policy of integration with the West, became a liberal democracy.

A distinct feature of the FRG is its federal structure. Until unification in 1990 it was comprised of 11 states called *Länder* (including West-Berlin). United Germany today has 16 Länder. Each *Land* has its own parliament, elected in state elections taking place every four or five years. The German constitution gives the *Länder* certain rights, more specifically legislative authority in certain areas that the states exercise independently of the federal level. Most importantly, the *Länder* have legislative authority over everything concerning culture, including the mass media, as well as education (schools, universities) and the police. Conversely, this means that the national state has no authority in these areas or is restricted to defining guidelines that are then turned into law at the state level. Moreover, the *Länder*, based on the size of their population, are represented in the *Bundesrat* (Federal Council), one of two chambers taking part in the legislative process at the federal level.

The national parliament is the *Bundestag*. Until the parliament moved to Berlin at the end of the 1990s, its seat had been in Bonn that served as provisional capital of West Germany. From 1961 until unification the *Bundestag* had 496 seats (plus 22 from West Berlin, counted separately due to the special status of the city). The number of seats increased to 656 with the integration of the East German *Länder* in 1990 but was reduced again to 598 with the election of 2002.

While the president is the head of state, his function is mainly representational. The post of chancellor is de facto the most important office in the German political system. The chancellor is elected by parliament by majority vote. As absolute majorities for one party are rare exceptions, coalition governments are the rule in Germany. To be elected chancellor, therefore, a candidate usually requires the support of two parties. The chancellor proposes the members of the government, the ministers, who are then formally appointed by the German president. Consequently, the ministers are dependent on the chancellor but not on parliament. The chancellor is the one who determines and is responsible for the direction of government policy and thus stands "above" the ministers. Owing to the chancellor's strong position, the German system has also been called a "chancellor democracy." A government can only be unseated by a vote of no-confidence against the chancellor. In taking this step, parliament has to find a majority for a new chancellor. Hence, a successful vote of no–confidence pushes the chancellor and all ministers out of office.

The development of the German electoral system

The first parliamentary elections were held in August 1949, three months after the new constitution was adopted, which guaranteed free and equal elections by secret ballot. In addition, the constitution assigned the parties a decisive role in the political system by expressly stating that they should contribute to the formation of the political will.

The parties were either newly founded or restored soon after the end of the war. The Social Democratic Party (SPD) can trace its roots back to the 19th century. It had been banned during the "Third Reich" but nevertheless was able to build upon its Weimar experience as soon as Germans were allowed to resume political activities after the war. The conservative Christian Democratic Union (CDU) officially came into existence in 1950, when the

Christian Democrats, until then organized only at the state level, united nationally. The CDU forms a permanent coalition with the Christian Social Union (CSU), which only puts up candidates in the state of Bavaria where the CDU itself is not represented. The Free Democratic Party (FDP), positioned at the center of the political spectrum, was formed in 1948 when the state associations of the Liberal Party united. For a long time the FDP was only the other party besides the SPD and CDU/CSU successfully established in the German party landscape (or an overview of German parties, see e.g., Jesse, 1997; Niedermayer, 1997).

The Parliamentary Council, convened to write the Basic Law, proposed the adoption of a personalized proportional electoral system, with one part of the parliamentary representatives elected according to a majority system and the other part according to a proportional system. The electoral system, however, was not laid down in the constitution. This was a direct result of experiences made in the Weimar Republic (1918–1933), during which time the electoral system had been fixed in the constitution. This had made changes possible only with a two-thirds majority which could never be reached because of the fragmentation of the parties in the Weimar parliament (*Reichstag*).

The first national elections in post-war Germany were held under a Federal Election Law announced in the summer of 1949. Officially at that point, laws were to be issued by the allied military governors but, in some cases, they delegated this right to the heads of the state governments. The Parliamentary Council, however, whose task had been restricted to writing the new constitution, went ahead and proposed its own election law. While this caused some dispute with the Allies, the different parties represented on the Parliamentary Council were also in disagreement about the future electoral system. Only the smaller parties had a clear stance on the matter. They feared that a majority system would leave them with no seats in parliament, so they favored a proportional system. The big parties preferred the majority system instead. The SPD, however, finally decided to back a proportional system, at least for the first federal elections, arguing that a majority system would bring about a political polarization unhealthy for the young democracy. The CDU/CSU, on the other hand, rejected the electoral law, even though the proposal of the Parliamentary Council offered a compromise by mixing elements of the proportional and majority systems, but they were outvoted. When the electoral law was finally announced in June 1949, it was a true exercise of compromise between the Parliamentary Council, the Allies, and the *Länder* premiers, who the Allies had brought into the discussion after the Parliamentary Council had made its proposal. A certain bias in favor of a proportional system can be seen in the fact that several *Länder* had already adopted such an electoral system (Görtemaker, 1999, pp. 75–78; cf. in more detail Lange, 1975, pp. 329–408).

Under the electoral law of 1949, 60 percent of the 400 seats in the *Bundestag* were to be determined by direct vote for a candidate in 242 single-member constituencies. The other 40 percent of the representatives would get their seats through a party list. At that time voters only had a single vote. This vote had to be given to a candidate, but at the same time, it counted as a vote for the candidate's party. The total number of seats each party received in the *Bundestag* depended on the percentage of the vote obtained by the party, calculated on a state-by-state basis. The number of direct mandates earned were subtracted from the total number of entitled seats, and the remaining seats were filled from the party list. If a party received more direct mandates than the total number of seats it was entitled to, these surplus mandates could be kept. This led to a higher number of seats than the planned 400 in the *Bundestag* (Recker, 1997, p. 268). Thus, German elections have been based on a personalized proportional system since 1949. This particular configuration of a "mixed-member proportional system" has also become known as the "German model" (Nohlen et al., 2000, p. 356).

The political structures in the new German state were designed against the background of experience brought in from the first democratic period in Germany, the Weimar Republic. Many of the politicians who influenced Germany's reconstruction after the war had already been active in politics before the Nazis took over in 1933, or were at least old enough to remember the problems of the Weimar time. The party system had been highly fragmented and many small parties had been represented in the *Reichstag*, keeping the parliament from functioning effectively. Preventing a similar situation in the *Bundestag* was one of the objectives of the new electoral system. Contrary to a previous decision in the Parliamentary Council, which would have given the smaller parties a considerable share of the votes, the state premiers added a threshold clause to the electoral law, stipulating that a party needed at least 5 percent of the votes in one *Land* or one direct mandate in order to be allocated any seats in the national parliament.

The CDU/CSU won the election in August 1949 by a margin of only 1.8 percent ahead of the SPD. With two surplus mandates, the overall number of seats in the new parliament was 402. These seats were allocated to ten parties which had either attained more than 5 percent of the votes in one *Land* or at least one direct mandate. Evidently, the threshold intended to avoid party fragmentation was not yet working as well as expected. In fact, analysts would later regard the 1949 election as a transition from Weimar to Bonn, calling it the last Weimar election as well as the first election of the new Federal Republic. Voting behavior in 1949 showed the same cleavages that had been apparent in 1933. This would only change with the next election in 1953 (Falter, 1981).

One month after the election, the *Bundestag* elected CDU party chairman Konrad Adenauer as chancellor. He received 202 of the 402 votes, just one more—which was his own—than needed. He formed a coalition government of CDU/CSU, FDP, and Deutsche Partei (DP), a conservative party founded in 1947, mainly representing agrarian interests. The FDP won 11.9 percent of the vote, the DP 4 percent.

The number of competing parties increased even more after the Allies first relaxed and finally in early 1950 abolished the obligatory license for political parties. This, and more particularly the success of a new extreme right-wing party, started a public discussion about the need to change the electoral system to a majority system or to increase the 5-percent threshold. The CDU/CSU, again in favor of a majority system, now had to consider the interests of its smaller coalition partners in the government. They feared being wiped out by a polarization toward the two big parties. The SPD preferred instead a model similar to the one used for the election in 1949.

Many different proposals were made by all sides until the new election law passed the *Bundestag* in June 1953, a scant three months before the next election was scheduled. This law adhered to the same general principles as the one of 1949 but brought in some important changes. From now on each voter had two votes.

The first vote was given to a candidate in the constituency, the second to a party list. The overall number of regular seats in the *Bundestag* was raised to 484. The ratio of direct mandates to seats obtained by the party list was changed to 50:50. A direct mandate was achieved by plurality, but it was still the party vote that determined the strength of a party in parliament, thus cementing proportionality as a defining characteristic of the German electoral system. Also in 1953, the 5-percent clause was broadened. Parties now needed at least 5 percent of the vote in the entire country and not just in one *Land*, or at least one direct mandate before being represented in parliament (Nohlen, 2000, p. 306).

With about 45 percent of the votes, the CDU/CSU won a clear majority in the 1953 election, while the SPD only received 28.8 percent. Chancellor Adenauer formed a coalition government with the FDP, DP, and GB/BHE (Gesamtdeutscher Block/Block der Heimatvertriebenen und Entrechteten), a party representing expellees and war refugees. This coalition gave Adenauer the two–thirds majority in the *Bundestag* he needed to make changes to the constitution, such as the ones necessary to re-establish and reform the German army. Also, by including the small parties in the government, Adenauer hoped to strengthen their will to cooperate with the Christian Democrats at the *Länder* level as well. He needed their support to get laws requiring second-chamber consent through the *Bundesrat* (Lange, 1975, p. 591). The small parties, on the other hand, hoped to wrap up the electoral law issue before the planned constitutional changes came to vote.

Smoldering conflicts among the parties of the coalition government were fueled by an election law proposal put forward by the CDU/CSU at the end of 1955. It would have favored the Christian Democrats and put both the smaller parties and the SPD at a disadvantage. The proposal was based on a so-called gap electoral system which would have combined the proportional system with a majority system. The "gap" came about by actually separating the two votes: One half of the members of parliament were to be elected by the first vote in the constituencies according to a majority system. The other half were to be elected through a party list based on the second vote (Lange, 1975, pp. 634–636).

In particular, the FDP threatened to leave the coalition, a step that also led to a certain rapprochement between the Liberals and the SPD. New alliances at the level of the *Länder* were discussed.

In early 1956, the coalition in North Rhine-Westphalia, the largest *Land* in Germany by population, fell apart and was replaced by a new government made up of the SPD, the FDP, and the catholic Zentrum party. The ongoing conflicts in Bonn were the main reason for this break up.

When the new election law finally passed the *Bundestag* in March 1956, it had only undergone minor changes from the law used in the last elections. While the calculation of seats had previously been done for each *Land* separately, it was now done on the basis of the entire country. Hence, the overall number of second votes given to a party now decided the number of seats it got in the *Bundestag*. The prohibitive clause was amended again. Parties now required either 5 percent of the overall vote or three direct mandates to enter the *Bundestag*. These innovations from 1953 of giving each voter two votes and applying the 5-percent threshold to the number of votes obtained in the entire country remain important defining characteristics of the German electoral system. In addition, the 50:50 ratio of seats gained through direct mandates and party lists has stayed the same since 1953.

It was mainly the FDP that had been interested in increasing the number of direct mandates needed to enter parliament. The party was sure that it could make the thresholds but hoped that the other small parties would fall by the wayside. This could be regarded as the first step in the party's strategy of establishing itself as the "third power" between the two big parties. The prevention of a one-party government thus became an important political argument of the FDP. Over the years, the party became accustomed to tipping the scales either in favor of the CDU/CSU or the SPD.

After the new electoral law had passed both chambers of parliament, the small parties, fearing that these hurdles were too high for them, started initiatives at different levels to amend the law again. Several complaints were filed with the Federal Constitutional Court. However, the court upheld the thresholds as an instrument for preventing party fragmentation in parliament. Amendments tabled in the *Bundestag* also failed. At last, the small parties sought pre-election agreements over constituencies with the other parties and, at the same time, initiated merger negotiations. These were successful only in two cases and were still no assurance of making it over the entry hurdles.

With these changes in place for the third round of parliamentary elections in Germany after the war, the electoral system had taken its final shape and was not changed again. However, the discussion on electoral law came up again during the 1960s with the prospects of a grand coalition and the possibility of a Social-Liberal coalition as a replacement to the long-lived Christian-Liberal coalition.

The first occasion during which the switch to a majority voting system seemed close at hand was in late 1962. After the *Spiegel* Affair, a scandal involving the German news magazine *Der Spiegel* and Franz Josef Strauß (CSU), then Minister of Defense, the FDP had withdrawn its ministers from the government. The FDP hoped to force the formation of a new government without Strauß. Strauß, however, had no intentions of resigning. A solution to this difficult situation emerged for Adenauer when the SPD proposed negotiations for a grand coalition with the CDU/CSU. The introduction of a majority voting system, which would have sooner or later meant the development of a two-party system, was among the issues the two sides had agreed upon. Both parties were aware that this would be the deathblow to the FDP. When Strauß declared that he would renounce his cabinet position and the SPD began to have reservations against a majority system, Adenauer once again turned to the FDP. Threatened by the introduction of a new electoral law, they were all too ready to re-enter the government. This decision was made even easier for the FDP since Adenauer complied with its wish and promised to step down in the summer of 1963, thus opening the way for his successor Ludwig Erhard (Görtemaker, 1999, pp. 383–385).

Erhard (CDU) was chancellor for only three years. After he lost the backing of his own party and four FDP ministers left his government, he was forced to resign in November 1966. Because of the discord between CDU/CSU and FDP, the two big parties took up negotiations which finally led to a grand coalition under the new chancellor Kurt Georg Kiesinger (CDU). During the negotiations the two parties agreed to introduce a majority system for the election in 1973 and to examine the possibility of applying an interim electoral system in 1969. There was a reason for discussing an interim voting system and further strengthening the entry thresholds: The extreme-right National Democratic Party (NPD) had been making inroads in recent *Länder* elections. These plans were soon scrapped, however, as they smacked all too much of manipulation.

While the CDU/CSU, optimistic about their electoral prospects for 1973, held on to the plan of introducing a majority voting system, doubts arose in the SPD about its own ability to ever ascend to power without the support of another party. Not wanting to shut the door on a Social-Liberal coalition completely, the SPD broke their coalition agreement with the CDU/CSU and put off the decision on the introduction of a majority voting system until the next legislative period. While Kiesinger wanted to continue the grand coalition regardlessly, Willy Brandt (SPD), the vice-chancellor and Minister of Foreign Affairs at the time, was already eyeing a new coalition after the 1969 election. The FDP, feeling they had been saved by the SPD, was ready for the new constellation (Görtemaker, 1999, pp. 457–461). Even though the CDU/CSU came out of the election as the strongest party, almost winning an absolute majority, Willy Brandt formed a coalition government with the FDP and was elected chancellor in October 1969. Changing the electoral system was no longer an issue, and never has been again, at least not amongst the parties. The only further change to the system was made in 1985 when the method of allocating seats was switched from the D'Hondt divisor system, which works to the advantage of the bigger parties, to a quota system. Since the 1987 *Bundestag* elections, parties have been allocated seats according to the Hare/Niemeyer formula (cf. Mackie, 2000), which is slightly more advantageous for the smaller parties.

The discussions of the voting system, spanning nearly two decades, reveal strategic thinking on all sides and the readiness of the parties to use the voting system as an instrument to advance their own interests. Each party's stance on electoral law was very much determined by calculations of own advantage and by the presumed need of a future coalition partner.

With only three parties represented in parliament until the Greens appeared on the scene and made it into the *Bundestag* in 1983, the FDP, though only a small party with usually less than 10 percent of the vote, enjoyed a position of power as the coalition maker for both big parties. In fact, with the exception of the 1957–1961 legislative period and the three years of the grand coalition (1966–1969), the FDP was excluded from the government the first time in the post-war years in 1998 when a coalition of the SPD and the Greens took over.

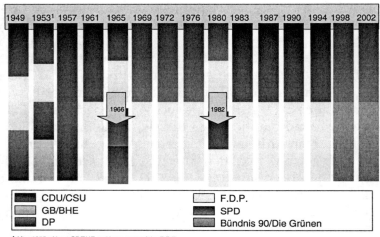

Figure 1: German governments 1949–2002

Split-votes and surplus mandates

Since the electoral law was amended in 1953, each German voter has had two votes, dubbed the first and second vote. The first vote is given to a candidate in the voter's constituency, the second vote goes to a party. Because the number of seats that an individual party gets in parliament is based on the second vote, the second vote is more important and actually the decisive vote, although the term suggests otherwise.

The availability of two votes allows for split-voting. Contrary to the use of the term in the United States, in Germany a split-vote means voting for a candidate from one party with the first vote and then voting for another party with the second vote. The percentage of split-votes has risen considerably over the last 20 years (Figure 2). Until the mid-1970s the numbers of split-votes remained under 10 percent. The share of split-votes exceeded 10 percent for the first time in the 1983 *Bundestag* elections, and since then has risen to a high of 20 percent in 1998.

Various factors could explain this trend. Recent research on split-voting characterizes split-voters as being mainly young people and those with a higher educational level and a higher level of political interest. These findings lend support to the assumption that the general rise in the level of education and the growing interest in politics that went hand in hand with it, are among the factors that explain the tendency to split the votes.

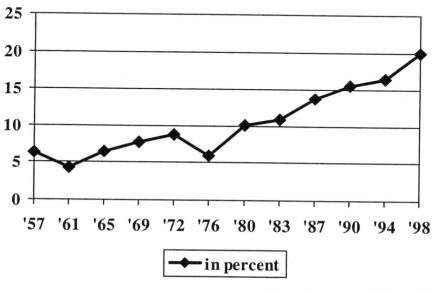

(Hilmer & Schleyer, 2000, p. 193)

Figure 2: Split-voting at *Bundestag* elections 1957–1998

Another reason may be that split-voting has become a subject of public debate. The second-vote strategy of the FDP has made split-voting a campaign issue which other parties reacted to and which also made the topic a media issue (cf. Chapter 4 in this book). Still another reason for the rising numbers of split-voters is seen in the fact that during the same time period the number of parties running for election has increased. While in 1976 16 parties entered the electoral battle, there were 40 parties running in 1998 (Hilmer & Schleyer, 2000, p. 174). Among them are mostly very small groups, with minimal chances of success, particularly at the constituency level. Therefore these parties often do not nominate candidates, or at least not in each constituency. This forces their voters to split their vote or to forfeit one of their two votes (Hilmer & Schleyer, 2000, p. 174). Finally, the development of a two-bloc system with the Christian Democrats and the Liberals on one side and the Social Democrats and the Greens on the other has been put forward as a reason for the increase in split-voting (Jesse, 1988, p. 115). Voters, although preferring one of the big parties may want to support the smaller party of the bloc in order to increase the chances for a particular coalition. However, together with the general weakening of party identification and the increasing number of floating voters, split-voting has been regarded as one characteristic of the unpredictable voter who represents a challenge to the parties and their campaign efforts.

There has also been a discussion of whether split-votes are an act of rational or tactical voting or rather sincere voting. In splitting a vote, the rational voter may consider a party's or candidate's chances at overcoming the thresholds as well as likely coalitions (e.g., Schoen, 1998). When casting the first vote, the rational voter can take into account a candidate's chances of winning the constituency and thus receiving a direct mandate for the *Bundestag*. In Germany, most constituencies are won by the candidates of the two big parties. Only in a few cases have popular candidates of the smaller parties won a majority over their competitors. According to the wasted-vote thesis, as adopted from Duverger (1963) and adapted to the German electoral system, e.g. by Fisher (1973), voters of smaller parties may therefore decide to give their first vote to the candidate of one of the big parties instead of wasting it.

When casting the second vote, the rational voter has to consider the probability that a party will make it over the five–percent hurdle and obtain seats in the *Bundestag*. This decision is particularly difficult in a situation when the party is oscillating around 5 percent and might very well miss the threshold by only a slight margin. In addition, the rational voter can consider a possible coalition for the new government on the basis of her/his party preference. Such a voter might therefore decide to cast their ballot for a small party in order to help it over the five-percent hurdle and make the party available for a preferred coalition. Thus, the availability of two votes in the German electoral system allows for tactical voting if the necessary information can be obtained by the voter.

Because this kind of tactical voting requires knowledge of the electoral system, the capability to estimate the strengths of the parties and candidates, and involves high costs for obtaining the information needed for a tactical decision, some authors have argued that splitting the votes is more an indication of sincere voting. Sincere voters are guided by different preferences when casting their first and second votes, but may not be acting "rationally" in the sense of tactical voting (Nohlen, 2000; Thurner, 1999).

This position is supported by the finding that many German voters do not understand the meaning of the first and second vote. While survey data show that voters learn about the availability of two votes during the election campaign, most still regard the first and second vote as being equally important. In early August 1998, about seven weeks before election day, 94 percent of the Germans (16 years and older) knew that they had two votes in the election. However, two thirds of these respondents accorded the same importance to the first and second votes. The other third was almost equally divided between those who regarded the first vote as more important and those who regarded the second vote as having more weight (Allensbacher Archiv, 1998).

A study examining the correlates of knowledge of the electoral system found a clear relation between intensive use of the mass media, in particular the use of political information, and a stable knowledge of the meaning of the two votes. Interestingly, a longer experience with elections, measured by the age of voters as an indication of the number of *Bundestag* elections a voter could have participated in, as well as coming from a *Land* with the same electoral system as at the federal level, did not give voters a better knowledge of the meaning of the two votes (Schmitt-Beck, 1993).

The phenomenon of surplus mandates is closely connected to each voter having two votes. These surplus or excess mandates are acquired by parties that win more direct mandates in a *Land* than they are entitled to according to the percentage of second votes. Dependent on the number of surplus mandates all parties reach in an election, the number of seats in the *Bundestag* can be higher than is determined in the electoral law.

Over the years, the number of surplus mandates has remained small. In some elections, no surplus mandates were gained at all. While the election in 1990 produced six surplus mandates, that number rose to 16 in 1994. The CDU alone gained 12 of these surplus mandates. Given that the Christian-Liberal coalition only had a small majority based on the second vote percentages, the surplus mandates secured the coalition a more comfortable majority.

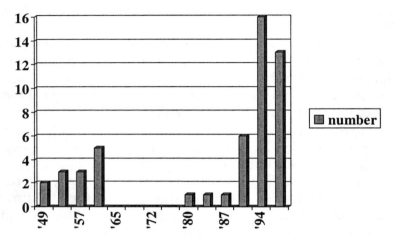

Figure 3: Surplus mandates 1949–1998

The high number of surplus mandates in 1994 raised discussions about their constitutionality because they change the outcome of the proportional system. In a decision brought down in April 1997, the Federal Constitutional Court used the five–percent hurdle to point out that the proportional system is not in any detail the guiding principle of the German electoral system and confirmed the permissibility of surplus mandates as a consequence of the personalized element of the voting system (Nohlen, 2000, pp. 324–325). However, the Court asked the legislators to limit the number of surplus mandates, suggesting 5 percent as a threshold. In 1998, the number of surplus mandates was 13, this time all won by the SPD.

The electoral thresholds

Since the first post-war election, thresholds have been a characteristic of the German electoral system. The decision in favor of a threshold in the new election law was very much due to the experience of the Weimar Republic. The fragmented party structure that was mirrored in the *Reichstag* was one of the reasons for the instability of the Weimar governments and their short life span. The thresholds introduced with the election law of 1949— 5 percent of the votes in one *Land* or one direct mandate— were thought sufficient to prevent such a situation in the new democracy. However, when ten parties managed to enter parliament after the first elections, it became clear that these thresholds had not shown the expected effectiveness. In the 1953 election, the five-percent hurdle was broadened by requiring parties to obtain 5 percent of the vote at the national level and not just in one *Land*. Because regional strongholds made it comparatively easy for small parties to win one constituency and thus get into the *Bundestag*, the minimum number of direct mandates needed to bypass the five-percent hurdle was raised to three for the 1956 election.

In fact, over the years the thresholds have had concentration effect. Whereas ten parties made it into the *Bundestag* after the first federal elections in 1949, seemingly harking back to the chaos of Weimar, only six parties were represented in the second *Bundestag* elected in 1953. The number of parties shrank to four with the election in 1957. Although it was mainly the CDU/CSU that absorbed the smaller parties and their voters, the SPD has also steadily increased its share of the vote over the years. Since the 1950s the overwhelming majority of the votes has thus gone to the big parties. Their combined share of the votes was above 80 percent since 1957 and even greater than 90 percent during the 1970s. With the advent of the Greens as a fourth party on the scene, the CDU/CSU and SPD saw their share of the vote drop somewhat. It finally fell below 80 percent in 1990 when the PDS successfully made its way into the *Bundestag*. Nonetheless, the big parties together still account for more than three quarters of all votes.

For a long period, the FDP was the only party able to carve itself a place in the political landscape. The party may be small, seldom obtaining much more than ten percent of the vote and often much less, yet it successfully prevented the development of a two-party system in Germany. Only in 1957 did one of the big parties reach an absolute majority. In order to form a majority government in the *Bundestag*, the big parties have otherwise needed a coalition partner. The FDP has made a strategy of propagating itself as "the third force," as a counterbalance to the big parties, necessary to prevent a one-party government or a grand coalition of the two. This argument has proven good against both the CDU/CSU and SPD and can be used to justify a coalition with either party. After a long-term partnership with the Christian Democrats during the 1950s and 1960s, except for the 1957–1961 legislative period and a short time in the opposition during the years of the grand coalition (1966–1969), the Liberals changed sides and in 1969 became the junior partner in a Social-Liberal coalition. The party switched back to the CDU/CSU when the tide turned for SPD chancellor Helmut Schmidt and differences in the economic programs of both parties seemed unbridgeable. The FDP acted as the agent of the "political turn" in 1982 by helping the Christian Democrats back into government, this time under the chancellorship of Helmut Kohl (CDU).

The three-party system, with the FDP always playing a decisive role despite its size, did not change until the early 1980s when the Greens appeared on the scene. In the 1983 federal election, the party overcame the five-percent hurdle and entered the *Bundestag* for the first time. The establishment of the Greens changed the rules of the political game by opening up new coalition possibilities and weakening the position of the FDP. Now two parties could offer themselves as a corrective force to the power of the big parties. However, coming as an addition on the left side of the political spectrum, ideological differences between Greens and Christian Democrats seemed to make a partnership of Greens and SPD the only new alternative. Thus, during the 1990s the political landscape in Germany developed into a two–bloc system with the Christian Democrats and the FDP on one side, and the SPD and the Greens on the other. However, it was not until 1998 that the Greens and the Social Democrats were strong enough to form a coalition government and send the CDU/CSU and FDP into the opposition.

At the same time, a fifth party made it into the *Bundestag*. After the dissolution of the political system of the German Democratic Republic in 1989, the former GDR state party, the SED (Socialist Unity Party of Germany), changed its name to the Party of Democratic Socialism (PDS) and more or less adapted its ideology to the new realities of unified Germany. The party has maintained a strong position in the East with impressive electoral success in the new *Länder* but has hardly gained a foothold in the West.

The first all-German elections after unification were scheduled for early December 1990. A special Election Treaty increased the number of *Bundestag* seats from 518 to 656. The Treaty also applied the five-percent hurdle to the entire country; however, the Federal Constitutional Court declared this to be unconstitutional. The Court argued that under the special conditions of the first post–unification elections, the five-percent threshold, if calculated based on the national voting percentages, would work to the dis-advantage of the East German parties. Consequently, the decision was made to treat East and West Germany separately. As a result, the five-percent hurdle was not calculated at the national, all-German level, but rather based on the votes obtained in either the West or in the East. This regulation saved the Greens, who fell short of the necessary 5 percent in the West. However, their sister party in the East, Bündnis 90/Die Grünen, received 6 percent of the votes in East Germany, which gave the Greens representation in the *Bundestag*. The PDS, in the same situation, obtained more than 11 percent of the votes in the East and entered the *Bundestag* in 1990.

That transitional ruling lapsed in 1994 and parties now need 5 percent of the vote across the entire country to enter parliament, which puts the PDS with its strongholds in the East at a disadvantage. Nevertheless, the party has continuously been represented in the *Bundestag*. In the 1994 federal elections, although it only obtained 4.4 percent of the vote, the PDS succeeded in winning four direct mandates, one more than it needed to make it into parliament. In 1998, not only did its share of 19.5 percent of the vote in the East work out to an all–German average of 5.1 percent, the PDS successfully defended the four direct mandates won in 1994.

Thus, as intended, the electoral thresholds in Germany have prevented the development of a fragmented party system. The small parties that were active in the early years of post–war Germany could not survive and disappeared from the political scene, being absorbed in part by their bigger competitors. For about two decades, until the early 1980s, the German party system was a three or rather a two–and–a–half party system. While the SPD and CDU/CSU have dominated the political process and the chancellor has always been from one of these parties, the third party, although much smaller, has constantly played a decisive role by helping one of the big parties to power. With the appearance of the Greens and their successful entry into the *Bundestag* in 1983, the FDP now has a competitor when it comes to tipping the balance of power. This new option, however, only seems open to the SPD. Ideological differences would appear to make a coalition between the CDU/CSU and the Greens impossible in the near future. The establishment of the PDS as a fifth party at the national level differs from the appearance of the Greens. While the Greens brought new issues into the political discussion, the PDS has based its success on its roots in East Germany and by presenting itself as the only party that represents the East and understands the East German mentality and problems.

As another addition to the left of the political spectrum, the PDS could cooperate with the SPD, an option which has indeed been realized in some state parliaments in the East and in Berlin, where the PDS even managed the five-percent hurdle in the West–Berlin districts in the 2001 elections. A coalition with the PDS at the national level, however, is not to be expected in the near future because of the party's past and the problems that collaboration with the PDS would cause for their partners, particularly in West Germany.

The German electoral system as a model?

"Discussions about the electoral system are discussions about power" (Nohlen, 2000, p. 60). The early efforts to reform the electoral system in Germany confirm this statement. The parties, the small ones just as much as the big ones, fought the fight in their own interest. The reactions that each proposal for electoral system change provoked from the parties not only demonstrated the difficulties of a reform but soon made it clear that change was almost impossible. Since changes proposed to the electoral system almost always reflected a party's own interests, any modifications smacked of manipulation. As a result, once the electoral system had taken its final shape along the lines proposed by the Parliamentary Council, it became a matter too delicate to touch again.

The "German model" and its combination of the proportional system with a personalized element has sometimes been praised as a model for other countries (cf. Nohlen, 2000, p. 326). Its adoption, for example by New Zealand and Venezuela, seems to support this view. The fact that voters have two votes, misleadingly named first and second votes, even though the second is the more important of the two, makes the German electoral system somewhat complicated and has prompted some researchers to plead for simplification. On the other hand, the small percentage of invalid votes does not lend support to calls for change. So even if voters have to learn the meaning of the two votes anew in every election, and even though many still do not exactly know what they are doing when they cast their votes, the German model works. As far as its degree of proportionality is concerned, the German electoral system achieves high scores (cf. Lijphart, 1999, p. 162; Powell, 2000, p. 96) despite its comparatively high threshold.

Chapter Two

New Zealand: The Popular Overthrow of an Electoral System

From 1853 until 1996 New Zealand's electoral system was a close replica of the British Westminster plurality model. Indeed, New Zealand arguably provided a better example of the Westminster model than did Britain because of its largely exclusively two–party system, its concentration of executive power in single party cabinets, and its extreme interest group pluralism (Lijphart, 1999). Yet New Zealanders effected a move away from their apparently entrenched electoral system toward one of proportional representation. The move, an internationally rare occurrence, was ultimately reflective of power struggles between citizens, their elected representatives, and sectional interests. This chapter describes the events surrounding and the nature of those struggles.

From the 1970s New Zealanders had become increasingly dissatisfied with the performance of successive governments and much of that dissatisfaction could be related to issues of representation. After decades of strong party loyalty, largely divided on socio–economic lines, voters had become less inclined toward loyalty to any one political party as they sought instead to elect representatives whom they believed would support particular interests in policy formation (Vowles, 1995). This meant that the numbers of undecided voters increased, which, in turn, opened the way for support for minor parties even though the electoral system continued to deny those parties access to the political field as representatives. It also increased the likelihood that one of the two main parties (the National Party and the New Zealand Labour Party) would be elected to government without the majority of public support, thus putting pressure upon the electoral system.

In two successive elections, 1978 and 1981, the conservative National Party was re–elected to power with a majority of seats but without an overall majority of votes. The disproportional 1978 election result initiated a move toward proportional repre–

sentation; a recommendation also made in a book published in 1979 by a then new Labour MP and constitutional law expert who was later to become Prime Minister, Geoffrey Palmer (Palmer, 1987).

The election of governments without a strong voter mandate was exacerbated by the pursuit by those governments of radical and unpopular economic policies. In spite of its lack of popular support, and in the face of widespread opposition, the National Government of 1978–1984 pursued strongly interventionist policies while at the same time incurring enormous national debt by borrowing heavily in order to finance large energy–related projects (Bertram, 1997). In 1984, a Labour Government was elected with an overall majority vote. This time, however, the government turned away from its traditionally social democratic focus and introduced a series of radical, neo–liberal reforms which included the privatization of state–owned assets, the deregulation of finance markets, and the abolition of export and domestic subsidies (Kelsey, 1997). By 1990 there was widespread dissatisfaction with the government's economic policies.

The Labour Government itself was divided over its own policy direction, splitting shortly after its 1987 election victory when it became apparent that the Minister of Finance, Roger Douglas, supported by Treasury, intended the economic reforms to be extended to reforms in the social sector (Kelsey, 1997). The Prime Minister, David Lange, attempted to stall the program, but he resigned his position after disputes over Douglas's continued membership in the Labour Government Cabinet. The party was left in disarray having effectively discarded its traditional voter base and losing support from the newly wealthy business sector, largely because of the economic depression resulting from the 1987 stock market crash.

The National Party was re–elected to power in 1990, again with a disproportional election result. They won 69 percent of the Parliamentary seats but only 48 percent of the popular vote (Vowles, 1995). Voters expected that National would govern in a moderate, conservative way, and would slow the pace of the previous eight years' reform (see also Miller and Catt, 1993; Vowles and Aimer, 1993). Instead, however, the National Government extended the neo–liberal reforms, further reducing the welfare state and introducing the Employment Contracts Act that effectively removed power from trade unions. Furthermore, National reneged on its election promise of removing a surtax on government superannuation entitlements, a reversal that cost the party its traditional support of the conservative elderly (cf. Miller and Catt, 1993).

With each of the major parties having failed to represent the wishes of their traditional constituencies, New Zealand faced a crisis of representation. Who could voters identify with and trust to represent their interests in government? Because of this, and because of the repeated failure of the electoral system to deliver the government that had the greatest overall number of votes, the call for electoral reform gained widespread popular support. Although Labour, with Geoffrey Palmer now as Deputy Prime Minister, had set up a Royal Commission of Inquiry into the Electoral System, the majority of the two main political parties were against any move toward proportional representation, arguably, because such a system would dilute the power of a single party government.

The Royal Commission's 1986 report recommended a Mixed Member Proportional electoral system, commonly referred to as MMP, based upon the German proportional system. MMP would bring 120 elected representatives to New Zealand's unicameral Parliament, 65 of them constituency representatives, elected under a plurality or first–past–the–post system. These would include five special Maori districts to which Maori[1] voters can choose to belong. The remaining 55 representatives would be drawn from party lists as required to produce an overall result that is proportional to the number of party votes won by each party. Thus voters would be given two votes—one for their local electorate (or constituency) representative and one for their preferred political party. Before it could be allocated any list seats, a party would have to cross a threshold of 5 percent of the party votes. If a party did not reach the threshold, its votes would be discarded. The other way that a party could win Parliamentary seats would be by winning at least one electoral seat, in which case the party would be awarded, from its party list, an allocation that is proportional to its percentage of party votes and the need to cross the threshold is waived. One notable variation from the German system is that no chancellor is separately elected. Instead, the positions of Prime Minister and Deputy Prime Minister are negotiated between the parties that form the governing coalition. To date, the position of Prime Minister has automatically gone to the leader of the largest of the coalition parties.

The struggle for change

Agreement to have a referendum on electoral reform came initially only through an election promise made in error by Labour in 1987, followed by a promise by National in 1990, in order to accentuate Labour's failure to deliver the referendum. National did not believe that the referendum would deliver a mandate for change (Jackson, 1993).[2] Even the business sector, which had a vested interest in the ability of a single party government to implement rapid and radical economic reform, was slow to counter proposals for electoral change. The New Zealand Business Roundtable eventually commissioned a report, published in 1992, in support of first–past–the–post (Cowen et al., 1992). The authors of the report maintained that proportional representation would result in an under representation of the median voter in favor of minorities. It also argued that ideologically diverse parties in Parliament would be unable to negotiate efficient policy reform (see also Vowles et al., 1998).

The first referendum that was put to the New Zealand public in 1992 had, as recommended by the Royal Commission, the purpose of determining whether or not a second, binding referendum should be held on the issue of electoral reform. It asked two questions. The first asked voters to decide between the status quo and electoral reform; the second asked voters to choose one of four alternative electoral systems, in spite of the fact that the 1986 Royal Commission had strongly recommended that the MMP system be adopted. There was a suspicion that the alternatives were offered in order to make the decision more complex than it needed to be and, therefore, more difficult. MMP was the only one of the electoral systems, including first–past–the–post, that was supported by an organised public campaign, that of the Electoral Reform Coalition. The major political parties had clearly underestimated the call for reform. The referendum returned a result that was overwhelmingly supportive for both change (85 percent), and MMP (71 percent) (Levine and Roberts, 1993).

The binding referendum was held in 1993 to choose between MMP and first–past–the–post. This time each of the two options was fiercely defended in organised campaigns. Although the major political parties had previously expressed support for the status quo and stood to lose considerably in terms of influence from the introduction of proportional representation, they did not overtly engage in campaigning for either option for fear of further antagonising voters. They had, however, through insistence upon an increase in numbers of MPs from 99 to 120 under MMP but not under first–past–the–post, introduced a bias against reform as politicians were greatly distrusted and it was assumed that few voters would opt for more of them.

A group of business people whose interests lay in the unfettered continuation of neo–liberal economic policies led the campaign for first–past–the–post. A single party government with whom they could negotiate matters of public policy also, arguably, more efficiently served business interests than would a multi–party coalition. In terms of representation, the business sector believed that a powerful single party would more directly represent their interests in the political field without interference from minor parties who predominantly represented the interests of other groups. The business group set up the Campaign For Better Government (CBG), led by the CEO of New Zealand Telecom, Peter Shirtcliffe. Telecom was one of the state–owned enterprises that had been privatised under the neo–liberal reforms and which was now a major corporation. The Electoral Reform Coalition (ERC) continued to campaign for MMP.

The two campaigns leading to the 1993 referendum on electoral reform and the groups that organised them were very different from each other in many respects (see Roper and Leitch 1995). The CBG, as stated, was business led. They ran an expensive, well–funded, campaign by the business sector. Early in the campaign Peter Shirtcliffe targeted businesses and prominent individuals for funds (Anti–MMP, 1993), openly stating that he was "going unashamedly to the business community and the wealthy" (Booker, 1993). The CBG sponsored a public opinion survey on MMP and first–past–the–post and based their campaign upon its findings. The survey results, which were leaked to the media, identified which groups could be most effectively targeted and which arguments would best resonate with their concerns.

The arguments identified centered on the apparent anonymity of party list candidates chosen by party officials, the instability and inter–party conflict that would occur with an increase in numbers of politicians and political parties, the risk to the country's economic recovery, and the suggestion that countries that already operated under MMP were trying to get rid of it (McManus, 1993). The campaign featured anxiety–increasing and negative television advertisements with the themes of party lists and risk—especially to economic reform. As recommended in the market research report, the key target group was women. One CBG advertisement claimed that Italy had rejected MMP because it had been "responsible for decades of waste, corruption and Mafia control." In fact, Italy had never had the same electoral system as was proposed for New Zealand. As explained in Chapter Three, Italy had a very different and much more proportionally based system than that of the German model. A complaint against the CBG advertisement was upheld, but by that time the misleading message had served its purpose.

The ERC and its pro–MMP campaign were in stark contrast to the CBG. The group was led by a retired public servant, Colin Clark. Spokespeople included academics while other active members were people from a wide range of backgrounds. They had very limited resources for their campaign with all of their income derived from individual donations, generally worth less than $50 each (Colin Clark, personal communication, 1994). The ERC also had institutional support from a growing number of minor political parties, as well as from the New Zealand Council of Trade Unions whose membership had suffered as a result of the Employment Contracts Act. The campaign took a grass roots approach, using billboards, brochures, car stickers, and other stickers that were centrally produced and sold to local branches and individuals. Because the Coalition had been formed since 1986 and had since then been campaigning for electoral reform, its members were well informed about their cause. They set up a speakers' bureau to provide speakers for community meetings throughout New Zealand, a resource that was widely drawn upon. Because of the intensity and negativity of the CBG campaign, the ERC eventually produced its own radio and television advertisements, using freely donated production expertise, equipment, and volunteer actors. They borrowed money to pay for airtime, but the broadcasting frequency of ERC advertisements was approximately one sixth that of the CBG. The principle theme of the ERC campaign was "fair representation."

In spite of the intensity of the campaigns for first–past–the–post, as well as the efforts of government to increase the odds against change, the result of the 1993 referendum demonstrated continued, although reduced, support for electoral reform. The greatest support for MMP came from Maori, and also from women (Vowles et al, 1995). Both of these sectors stood to gain an increase in representation in the political field, with more Maori and more women expected to gain parliamentary seats from party lists. Although the result of the referendum was binding, the Electoral Act of 1993 included a requirement for a review of MMP and of the electoral system more generally to be held in 2000.

The general election, held simultaneously with the electoral reform referendum, returned the National Party to government with a very small majority and only 35.1 percent of the popular vote (Vowles, 1998). Over the following three years, as individuals and parties prepared for the change to proportional representation, several National MPs left the party to form their own minor parties, although retaining their parliamentary seats. Thus, National became a minority government, supported by very small minor parties. Under MMP, none of these parties would have been in government because they would not have either crossed the five–percent threshold or won an electoral seat. Even more significantly, their total percentage of the overall vote, including National's, was less than that won by Labour.

Once the introduction of proportional representation was inevitable, the business sector sought other means of influencing the policy direction of the country. Several key members of the Campaign for Better Government group became members of a new lobby group called ACT, an acronym for the Association of Consumers and Taxpayers. The group eventually became the registered political party Act (no longer an acronym) under the presidency of Roger Douglas, the Labour Minister of Finance who is widely held responsible for the 1984 neo–liberal economic reforms that became commonly known as "Rogernomics." Another former Labour MP and supporter of Rogernomics, Richard Prebble, later became Act's political leader and three leaders of the former CBG also became political candidates for the new party. Act's political manifesto was based upon a book written by Douglas entitled *Unfinished Business*, in reference to the program of economic reform that was, as stated above, interrupted by Labour in 1987.

A further means of potentially influencing policy decisions, albeit indirectly, is through financial support for a particular political party in the hope of enhancing the outcome of a preferred party's election campaign. Given that influence is generally the objective of making donations; a donor is more likely to be willing to donate to a party that has a strong chance of being a part of government. Thus, donors respond to poll ratings. If they are low the expense is questioned because of the low likelihood of a return in policy influence, even if that influence is strictly limited to access to senior politicians. In 2002, business leaders who acknowledged that the "Clark–led Labour Government has helped create a stable and healthy business environment" admitted that a reason for donating to Labour was a "pragmatic inclination to help Labour become the government in its own right this time with no dependence on small parties" (O'Sullivan, 2002).

There are legal restrictions on party donations in New Zealand. The Electoral Act of 1996 requires the disclosure of the identity of any person donating more than $10,000 to a political party, although the inclusion of the disclosure requirement was strongly contested. The then National Government was wary of enforced disclosure because it could stop people donating and raise the issue of state campaign financing. Although the law was passed, it contains loopholes that allowed parties in 1999 and 2002 to receive a considerable amount of their election funding from sources that were impossible to identify. Parties have to file annual returns to the Electoral Commission detailing contributions and the names of those who donate more than $10,000. However, multiple anonymous donations of less than $10,000 can be made by using different sources; large anonymous donations can be made through the use of trust funds (Oliver, 2002).

Regardless of the sources of funding, political parties are limited in the amount they can spend on election campaigning. Currently (2002) a New Zealand political party can spend $1 million on a general election campaign plus $20,000 for each electorate it contests. There is an allocation of funding made by the Electoral Commission according to the number of MPs a party has, its membership, and its level of public support, although the allocation system remains contentious and not immediately transparent. The money must be used for radio and television broadcasts—either for airtime or advertisement production. Parties cannot buy this advertising from their own funds, but they can pay for production costs. Ten parties in 2002 were also allocated free radio and television time for their opening and closing addresses.

In 2002 the Justice and Electoral Law Select Committee planned to investigate the possibility of limiting political parties solely to state financing, removing the avenue for private donations, but it was stalled by government's saying that electoral officials and staff should be concentrating on the election instead. The issue has not disappeared, however, and is likely to come up again (Oliver, 2002). The Chief of the Electoral Commission has expressed a desire to end anonymous donations to political parties, as well as to curb the use of trusts to disguise donations, so that there is more transparency.

Representation

The first general election in New Zealand to be held under MMP was in October 1996. Because of the greatly increased potential for minor parties to gain parliamentary seats, an unprecedented number (23) of political parties registered for the election.[3] However, only six parties had representatives elected to Parliament, either through single electorate wins or by crossing the party vote threshold. Probably because of a combination of the then current social dissatisfaction and the new electoral system, these six parties were spread across an ideological axis from left to right within the political field. In this way they represented a much wider range of opinions and interests than had been possible under first–past–the–post. In successive elections (1999 and 2002) the ideological spread of elected political parties in New Zealand has remained consistent, albeit with some changes amongst the minor parties.

In 1996, the right of the political field was represented by Act, as described above, while the left was represented by the Alliance. The Alliance was a coalition of small parties including the New Zealand Green Party, Mana Motuhake (a Maori Party), and New

Labour (formed by Jim Anderton who left Labour in protest at Labour's shift to the right in economic policy during the 1980s). The two major parties, Labour and National, claimed the center–left and center–right, respectively. The center ground was claimed by New Zealand First, although that claim was in many respects not valid. The sixth party, the United Party, was also positioned close to the center although its one elected MP, Peter Dunne, was more closely aligned to National than Labour.

The only significant change in representation in 1999 was in the Greens's split from the Alliance to run for election independently. The Greens's independence offers voters a further dimension, beyond left and right, in the special interest of the environment. The party does, however, have a policy platform that also encompasses issues of social justice in line with other parties of the left. By the time of the 2002 election the Alliance had further split with Jim Anderton forming a breakaway party, the Progressive Coalition, which is closely aligned to Labour. This time the National Party gained only 21 percent of the party vote, an unprecedented setback for a major party. Because of National's low level of support and the relatively high support for the minor parties, United Future and New Zealand First, this election has given New Zealand what can be described as its first truly multi–party Parliament, as intended under proportional representation. Representation, from an ideological perspective, also took an interesting turn in 2002 demonstrating that proportionality increases representation across the political spectrum. This time, New Zealand First was much more overt than it had previously been in campaigning from a right–wing perspective on the policies of immigration and crime. Because of the damaging split of the Alliance close to the election, however, it is often argued that the left of the political field was without true representation. The Greens, as stated already, had left–leaning policies but were publicised by the media largely as a single–issue party.

Voter confusion

In spite of a government–funded public education campaign about the significance of their two votes, many voters were still confused. Only about half (48 percent) of the voters understood that the party vote was the one that would determine which party would gain the most parliamentary seats and thus be in a position to form a government (Vowles, 1998).

The problem, which continues as it does in Germany, lies in the fact that of the voters who believe the two votes to be of equal importance or the electorate vote to be more important. Many have also expressed the likelihood that they would split their votes giving one to each of their two preferred parties. Because National and Labour, the largest parties, have greater numbers of, and more highly profiled, electorate candidates, voters who want to split their votes are more likely to give their electorate vote to their preferred main party and their party vote to a minor party. The voters appear to believe that splitting their votes in this way is a tactic to support the smaller parties while still allowing the major parties to take a dominant role in government. The reality poses significant problems for the major parties that, through a diminished number of party votes, stand to suffer a diminished influence in government with voters not getting the result they had intended. It is also a problem, naturally, for voters and this was particularly evident in 1996 when New Zealand First signed a coalition agreement with National, in spite of voters' general expectation that it would go into government with Labour.

By the time of the 1999 general election New Zealand voters had no greater understanding of the respective role and value of their two votes. Understanding was so poor that there was considerable concern that those who intended to split their votes, in the mistaken belief that their constituency vote was of equal or greater value than their party vote, would not, in effect, be voting for the government they wanted (Main, 1999; Vowles, 1998). By March 2002 understanding of the primary importance of the party vote stood at 38 percent, while 43 percent believed that the two votes were equally important (UMR Insight Limited poll, March 2002). Vote–splitting is not, however, carried out entirely naively. New Zealand voters made it quite clear in 2002 that they did not want Labour to succeed in its bid to govern alone as a majority party. Significant numbers of voters gave their party vote to a minor party in what appeared a deliberate, and successful, tactic to impose either a coalition or, as it turned out, reliance by Labour on a minor party for support outside of a formal coalition agreement. In doing so, voters reinforced their support for proportional representation and their reluctance to allow a political party to govern alone.

Voter disillusionment

Another key area of uncertainty for both voters and political parties, particularly in 1996, was the formation of a coalition government: On what terms would a coalition be formed? Which parties would cooperate and which would form the opposition? The confusion was increased when the election result gave the balance of power to the opportunist and centrist minor party, New Zealand First. With New Zealand First's support either National or Labour could have led a coalition government for the 1996–1999 term. It took nearly two months of separate but simultaneous and secret negotiations between New Zealand First and each of the two major parties before a coalition agreement was signed. When it happened voters once more felt disillusioned with their electoral system. New Zealand First had campaigned on a platform of being the only party that could get rid of National, and yet it enabled National to form a government again. Voters for New Zealand First primarily comprised two groups: Maori and the conservative elderly. Maori, who had traditionally voted for Labour, sought representation through New Zealand First's dominant Maori candidates and leadership. In New Zealand First the conservative elderly believed they had an opportunity to punish National for breaking promises about superannuation without actually having to vote for Labour. Regardless of their motivations, New Zealand First voters had generally believed— and had, arguably, been led to believe—that Labour and New Zealand First would govern together (Miller, 1998).

Further problems with New Zealand's first coalition government to be formed under the new electoral system occurred as nine MPs from the New Zealand First Party who had entered office from the party lists defected in 1998 to become independent members. Another high–profile defection that occurred in 1997 was that of an Alliance list candidate who repeatedly failed to appear when Parliament was sitting. She eventually left the Alliance, a party of the left, gave her proxy vote to the center–right National, and disappeared from public view. Her actions, and the negative public reaction to them, have made political parties much more cautious about whom they place on their lists.

The problems of unstable coalition government and party defections have been widely held responsible for the fact that less than a year after the first MMP election public support for the electoral system had dropped to as low as 30 percent (Hubbard, 1997). The Labour/Alliance coalition elected in 1999 sought to address the problem of defections with what became known as a "party–hopping" law requiring either a by–election if an electorate MP left a political party or replacement from the party list of a resigning list MP. The legislation was introduced as the Electoral Integrity Amendment Bill, designed to maintain proportionality in Parliament and, according to the Attorney General Margaret Wilson, to enhance public confidence in the integrity of the electoral system. The law is to be phased out after two parliamentary terms—at the election due to be held in 2005.

The Electoral Integrity Amendment Bill has always been controversial and decried by opponents as anti–democratic. The key reason for such criticism is that the bill is perceived as giving too much control to political parties because party leaders, with the support of two thirds of the party's MPs, will be able to apply to expel any MP whose actions, in the party's opinion, "distorts the proportionality of political party representation in Parliament." This is interpreted as giving power to political parties to dismiss anyone who does not support the party line, regardless of issues of conscience. Opponents also argue that the phenomenon of significant numbers of MPs changing parties is symptomatic only of adjustment to the new electoral system and that the MPs concerned would be punished by voters at the next election. Indeed, such defections have occurred primarily between 1993 and 1996 as the country prepared for the MMP and between 1996 and 1999 when MMP was implemented for the first time. In 1999 voters made their expectations of the system clear by refusing to re–elect any MP who had changed party between 1996 and 1999. Furthermore, New Zealand First was punished for failing to meet the expectation that it would form a coalition with Labour in 1996 by having its party vote drop from 13 percent in 1996 to below 5 percent in 1999. Maori returned their votes to Labour. New Zealand First's leader, Winston Peters, won his electorate seat by a very small margin and so was returned to Parliament.

Public support for the electoral system increased to about 50 percent in 1999, especially amongst Labour and Alliance voters (Smellie, 1999). The increase was largely attributed to the publicly demonstrated cooperation between these two parties (see Chapter Five). Meanwhile, the National Party attempted to capitalise on public uncertainty and disillusionment by making an election campaign promise that it would stage a new referendum on the electoral system without waiting for the results of the Commission of Enquiry already mandated for the year 2000. Because they lost the election, it was a promise they did not have to keep.

As the popularity of the newly elected Labour/Alliance coalition government rose in 2000, so did support for MMP. Nevertheless, the New Zealand Business Roundtable and the National Party continued to press for a referendum to decide the future of the system. Those who want the system to continue, they claimed rather ironically, have vested interests in doing so. Clearly, minor parties would not vote for such a referendum— thus, while National is the only major political party calling for it, the referendum will not take place. While government appears to be stable, helped by a stable economy, there seems little likelihood that voters will opt for further electoral change.

Popular opinion on the electoral system appears to directly reflect the current perception of the government's performance, and for this reason it fluctuates. It may well be that expectations of what proportional representation would deliver were unrealistic- ally high in the first place but those expectations were inextricably linked to government performance. Voters wanted greater and fairer representation in government. They also wanted government to be more accountable to voters' wishes in its performance. Thus, it is very easy to hold the new electoral system responsible when it is perceived that the government is to blame, for example, for a downturn in the economy. In fact, MMP has realised many of the expectations that were outlined in the 1986 Royal Commission report. With members of seven parties elected in each of the three elections held under the new system to date, proportionality has resulted in greater and fairer representation in Parliament that gives voice to a wider range of interests and ideologies. The numbers of Maori, women, and other ethnic group representatives in Parliament have grown. Governments have had to consult over legislation much more widely with their parliamentary colleagues than was ever necessary under first-past-the-post.

The transition to MMP has not been smooth and perhaps because of that New Zealand's experience of electoral reform may well serve as an interesting and useful example to other countries seeking change. While there are elements of the New Zealand socio-cultural, historical, and political situation that are unique, the issues surrounding representation of citizens' interests in the political field are not. The New Zealand experience was that of a small country: a British colony that had adopted many of the political institutions of the "mother" country. Yet its citizens have historically expected and demanded a relatively high degree of egalitarianism. It was the first country in the world to extend suffrage to women. Because of the processes of colonisation, common throughout the world, New Zealand's indigenous population is now a minority group. Furthermore, New Zealand now has an increasingly heterogeneous society with diverse immigrant cultures from Pacific islands, such as Tonga, Samoa, and the Cook Islands, as well as Asia, South Africa, and significant groups from Somalia and Eastern Europe, and special interest groups.

Although the party lists have not always been used as expected to increase diversity of representation (see Chapter Five), these diverse minority groups, as well as women, who have been greatly underrepresented, now have a greater opportunity for both participation and representation in government. Further-more, citizens demanded and achieved the right to elect a government that should, by virtue of an increase in the range of voices with legislative power, be more accountable to the public will in policy formation.

Notes:

[1] Maori are New Zealand's indigenous people.

[2] Other authors focus more on the detail of the events in New Zealand leading up to the demand for electoral reform. For example, see

Jackson, 1993; Miller and Catt, 1993; Vowles, 1995; Vowles and Aimer, 1993.

[3] It can also be argued that the number was deceptively large in comparison to first–past–the–post elections because, for the first time, all parties appeared on a national ballot form rather than one that was designed for local constituencies only (Aimer, 1998).

Chapter Three

Italy: Proportional Vote: The Last Refuge for the Old Party System?[*]

This chapter focuses on some significant facts that make up the complex history of the Italian political system created by the Republican Constitution of 1947. The pure proportional electoral system envisaged by the "founding fathers" on the underlying assumption that it was the most democratic mechanism to assure the representation of all popular interests lasted for 46 years and strongly contributed to shaping the country's political idio–syncrasy. Presidents, governments, and parties often appealed to the original spirit of the proportional rule and stood as its paladins when some political factions attempted to initiate a debate on its possible revision or update. There has been a near taboo on discussing an alternative system because of a sense of national pride in this system vis–à–vis the allegedly less democratic plurality systems of some other countries like the United Kingdom, France, and the United States.

To what extent this passionate defense of the proportional system was imbedded in a genuine belief in the superior level of democracy in proportional rule, or rather to a more secular, if unspoken, defense of the status quo is hard to judge. Perhaps there was a mix of both reasons, especially since the parties of the left defended proportional representation (PR) as a distinguishing policy in 1953 when the Christian Democratic Party, with overwhelming electoral support, attempted to introduce a majority premium into the system. The major resistance to any change came obviously from the smaller parties, which were afraid of being wiped away by thresholds. The bigger ruling parties (such as the Christian Democrats (DC) and the Socialists) changed their stances on this matter over time. In the early 1980s

---

[*] This chapter was written in collaboration with Laura Castiglioni.

eroding electoral support prompted them to create solutions that could assure a more solid control of parliamentary majorities. The ideology of PR being fully democratic was starting to give way in favor of the ideology of government stability. In fact, as illustrated below, one distinctive feature of the Italian version of pure proportionalism was its blame as a major factor for the extreme weakness of any government coalition.

It is useful to look at how PR had worked for almost five decades and yet suddenly had all its limitations revealed, bringing about a major reform. The plurality system (PL) fulfilled a seemingly widespread demand for tangible change, although a part of PR survived. It could not be otherwise, for the "proportional outlook" was, and still is, deeply rooted in Italian political culture. Several actors in today's political environment have shown themselves at different times to be keen to return to a situation where the representation of interests is not penalized by first–past–the–post mechanisms—which may disrespect the will of 49.9 percent of the voters. However, Italy has decided to experiment with a mixed PL–PR system but it is unclear if it will last as long as its predecessor. The general election of 2001 seems to have removed the reservations of the majority regarding the application of recent rules. The parties that make up the government coalition led by Silvio Berlusconi are, at present, all happy with the election results. This is not to say that they have espoused the PL rule forever. There are signs of growing tensions between the various components of the coalition that might foreshadow endings that are customary in Italian politics. Within the fragmented clusters of the parties of the opposition tensions surround the question of whether they should form a stronger (and possibly) winning coalition or retain their own traditional identities that are so well protected by the old proportional system.

Structural features of the Italian political system

Italy has a symmetric bicameral system. This means that the two Houses (the Senate or Upper House and Chamber of Deputies or Lower House) have equal powers, both in terms of confidence in the government and in the legislative activity; that is, proposal of new or modification of existing laws.

The only difference between the two Houses lies in the electoral law used to elect their members. Part of the electoral law is contained in the Constitution; another has the status of ordinary law. The Constitution dictates: the number of members in Parliament—630 Deputies, 315 elected Senators; the Upper House is to be elected on a regional basis; the eligibility for active vote (18 years old for the Lower House and 25 for the Upper House); the eligibility for passive vote (citizens who are at least 25 years old for the Lower House, while the limit is raised to 40 years of age for the Upper House); the division of seats among electoral districts; and the length of a legislature at five years.

In addition, the Constitution also states that all citizens eligible to vote are automatically registered to vote; that the Houses must be directly elected; that all votes count equally, and that voting must be free, secret, and personal; and that voting is a civic duty. All other aspects of the election of the two Houses (including the electoral formula) are regulated by an ordinary law, which is currently Law No. 277, approved August 1993. Italy has a so-called *rigid* Constitution, and amendments require a rather long procedure. An ordinary law can be amended with the simple majority of the two Houses. Despite the technical ease, no government could implement any electoral reform, since the discussion on an alternative electoral law always implied consideration of its effect on parties. Italy had, in the so-called First Republic, a hyper proportional electoral system. Deviations from it implied a less favorable situation for small parties. Since small parties supported most governments, no agreement could be found.

The old electoral law and the transition to the new one

The Lower and Upper Houses had two different electoral systems that underwent only minor changes during the 55 years of their application. The first national elections of the Italian Republic took place on April 18, 1948. The Chamber of Deputies (Lower House) was made up of 574 MPs on the basis of a proportional representation system with competing party lists and intra–party preference voting. Seats were distributed by the method of the largest remainders. For the Upper House, the election was based on a plurality rule, with 65 percent of a districts's votes required for victory (Katz, 1995, p. 96; Mudambi et al., 2001, p. 31). Each region was divided into a number of single–member districts and the voters of each district voted for a single candidate. The districts that had not been assigned by the PL rule were added up on a regional basis and assigned by the PR d'Hondt. The combination of a very high threshold and a multi–party system virtually proportionalized the electoral rule of the Senate (Fusaro, 1995, pp. 40–41).

The two electoral laws, despite looking quite different on paper, were similar in practice. Both electoral systems were hyper proportional (Shugart and Wattenberg, 2001, pp. 25–55) and very favorable to the representation of small parties (Katz, 1995, p. 96), which contributed to the extraordinary instability of Italian governments. (Italy had 47 governments from 1948 until 1994—during the period of the old electoral system.)

The first attempt to deviate toward a more majoritarian system was the temporary introduction, at the beginning of the 1950s, of a majority premium. However, only the 1953 elections were run with a majority premium because of the furious opposition of the parties of the left which succeeded in bringing about its removal in 1954. From this time on, any attempt to introduce modifications in the electoral law by amendments in Parliament was unsuc–cessful because of the mutual blockages across the entire party spectrum.

At the beginning of the 1990s a committee for referendum (COREL) was formed to submit a request for a set of abrogative referenda to modify the electoral law. Given the mounting climate of general dissatisfaction with the proportional system, which was blamed for government instability, party fragmentation, lack of public accountability, and political corruption (Norris, 1995, p. 7; Donovan, 1995, p. 48), a direct appeal to the electorate was the only viable solution to introduce reforms.

In June 1991, through a referendum, the electoral law for the Lower House was modified, by abolishing the intra–party multiple preference vote, while the Constitutional Court ruled out two further proposals which could have a stronger impact. Before the referendum, a voter could indicate on the ballot for the election of the Lower House up to four preferences within the list she or he voted for, but after the referendum the voter was allowed to indicate only one preference.

The referendum concerning preferential voting had remarkable support: 62.5 percent of the electorate turned out to vote and 95.6 percent of the voters approved the removal of the multiple preference vote. The success of the referendum motivated COREL to resubmit a slightly modified version of the two rejected proposals back to the Constitutional Court.

The referendum proposal submitted by the committee concerned the election of the Upper House and suggested the deletion of 11 words in the text of the electoral law. The effect of this small modification would be to revoke the 65–percent threshold for the direct election of a candidate in his or her single–member district and to modify the method of calculating the group totals on the basis of which the remaining seats (one quarter of the total) would be assigned by PR (Katz, 1995, p. 97). The first change would guarantee the election of three quarters of the Senators under the first–past–the–post system, and the second change would mean that only the votes of directly elected candidates would be subtracted from the group totals for the PR allocation, instead of all the votes cast in a single–member district.

In the meantime, Parliament, feeling the pressure of the referendum, tried to address the issue of institutional reforms by appointing an *ad hoc* committee that included members of both Houses: *Commissione Bicamerale per le riforme istituzionali*. This Bicameral Committee was appointed before the Constitutional Court's pronouncement on the referendum proposal. Some of its members were actually hoping for a negative verdict, while the majority was trying to figure which electoral system would give their party a better chance if the referendum was approved. A minority of its members would have preferred that the Bicameral Committee rewrite the electoral law before the referendum took place (Fusaro, 1995, p. 49).

The probability that the Bicameral Committee would reach an agreement before the referendum took place was indeed minimal, because of the conflicting interests of the parties represented and the sudden and fast changes in the political environment provoked by the *Tangentopoli* scandals. Most of the parties in Parliament were put under investigation and lost credibility in front of the voters, which made it difficult for them to predict their strength in the next elections and the effects of one or the other electoral law in the future.

In this climate of uncertainty the Constitutional Court finally declared the referendum proposal admissible and the referendum was called on April 18, 1993. The turnout was 77.1 percent and the votes in favor of the changes were a landslide of 90.3 percent. Italian public opinion had made its voice heard to the party establishment that had ruled the country for decades: an overwhelming majority demanded radical change. Consistent editorials in the press remarked on the gap between civil society and the "party–cracy" that had widened over the years.

After the referendum, the Upper House had automatically endorsed a new electoral law, applicable immediately, by which members of the Senate could be elected by a mixed–member electoral system, while the law for the Lower House remained unchanged.

The impossibility of ignoring the referendum result and restoring the PR rule in the Senate, as well as the concerns about the different composition of the two Houses, prompted Parliament to revise the electoral law of the Lower House to take into account the wishes of the majority. The necessity of revising the electoral system for the Chamber of Deputies opened the door to new discussions about the Senate as well. Despite appearances, the proposal to modify the Upper House law further was perfectly legitimate. Strictly speaking, the law resulting from the abrogative referendum could not in fact be considered the preference of the electorate. In fact, a referendum can be used in Italy only to revoke laws or their parts, and the approval of a referendum means simply that the status quo has been rejected by the voters but cannot be considered a binding expression of a popular preference for the alternative.

Two points had been debated extensively within the Bicameral Committee: the ratio of majority and proportional seats given a preference for a mixed electoral system and the formula to assign the majority seats. A general agreement was reached in Parliament that the majority principle was very important to aggregate parties, and hence all proposals suggested that at least 60 percent of the seats be assigned with some type of majority rule.

The new electoral law

After long and heated discussions in the Bicameral Committee and in the media, Parliament approved the new law on August 4,

1993. It was the first sign of a positive response of a political class decimated by judicial actions and, to a certain extent, intimidated by a strong wave of public opinion urging a dramatic turn in domestic political customs. The introduction of a large majority quota into the electoral system was that "turn" which was likely to meet the citizens' plea for change, even if not necessarily the panacea for the evils of the collapsing old political establishment.

The new electoral law maintained the different rules for the Chamber of Deputies and the Senate. In particular, while the electoral law for the Upper House remains very close to the one resulting directly from the referendum, the law for the Lower House is rather different and more complicated. The electoral law for the Senate prescribes the following:

- The Upper House is elected on a regional basis, according to the Constitutional dictate.
- The territory of each region (with the exception of the two smallest regions, Molise and Valle d'Aosta) is divided into a number of districts roughly equal to three quarters of the seats assigned to the region. A technical committee is appointed with the task of redesigning the shape and size of the districts and of preventing any attempt at gerrymandering.
- Candidates can be independent or form groups. Only the groups are eligible for the proportional allocation.
- Candidates for the Upper House can run in only one district and are not allowed to be candidates for the Chamber of Deputies.
- Voters receive one ballot, which displays the names of the candidates running for the district alongside the symbol of her/his party or group.
- The candidate who receives the highest number of votes in each single–member district is elected. The Regional Electoral Office determines the electoral quota of each group by adding the votes obtained by all the candidates belonging to the group within each region excluding those that have already been elected. The electoral quotas of each group are then used to calculate the number of seats they will obtain with the d'Hondt method. Within each region, given the number of seats won by each group, the

candidates of the group who had the best results in their constituency win the proportional seats.

The law for the election of the Chamber of Deputies contains the following rules:

- Italy is divided into 26 multi–member districts (*circoscri–zioni*) and 475 single–member districts (*collegiuninominali*). Each multi–member district is the sum of a number of single–member districts. Three quarters of the seats assigned to each district are allocated with the plurality rule, one quarter with the proportional rule.
- Each candidate running for a single–member district has to declare her/his affiliation to one (or more) of the lists competing for the proportional district. The affiliation will be used for the "unbundling" (*scorporo*) when counting the votes for the multi–member districts. (A candidate can be connected to many lists, but each list can be connected only to one candidate.) The affiliation pattern has to be the same for all the single–member districts belonging to the same multi–member district but could change across the multi–member districts. The competition in the multi–member districts is between lists, with no preference vote.
- Each voter receives two ballots. One is to vote for the single–member and one to vote for the multi–member district.
- In the single–member districts, seats are allocated according the first–past–the–post method with the candidate receiving the simple majority of the votes winning the seat, as in the Upper House.
- As for the multi–member districts, a threshold is applied: only parties receiving at least 4 percent of votes at the national level are entitled to receive seats.
- The allocation of the seats to each party list in a multi–member district is obtained with the Hare quota largest remainder method. The vote total is divided by the number of seats to be allocated and the number obtained is the national electoral quotient (*quoziente elettorale nazionale*). The total number of votes obtained by each party (national electoral quota) is then divided by the national electoral

quotient. This is the number of seats that each list obtains. If the sum of votes awarded is smaller than the total number of seats, the remaining seats are allocated to the parties with the largest remainders.

- At this stage the number of seats won by each list is only determined nationwide. At the district level, seats are assigned to each list according to the integer district quotients (*quozienti circoscrizionali interi*), obtained by dividing the sum of the district electoral quotas of all parties that reached the threshold in a given district by the number of seats to be allocated. The district electoral quota of each list is then divided by the quotient with the result being the number of seats to assign to each list.
- The seats not yet assigned at this stage are allocated to the parties that have the biggest decimals in the quotients.
- The candidates for each party will be declared elected in the same order as shown on the list. Candidates who win more than one seat have to decide which seat to accept and consequently vacate the seats in all the other districts in which they were elected.

Both systems are mixed electoral systems with the proportion of seats to allocate determined by different formulae: the plurality rule in allocating one part of the seats and the principle of compensation in the proportional allocation. It should be noted that in the Lower House it is quite easy to avoid the proportionalization of the results through unbundling. As Katz (1995) argues, parties who hope to win a seat in a single–member constituency could present a phantom list for the multi–member district (including, for instance, the same candidates running for the single–member district), declare an affiliation only to that list, and ask their voters to vote only for the other lists to which they are unofficially connected. The unbundling, in case of victory, would be applied to the phantom list only. Katz considers this practice a pure theoretical speculation and unlikely to take place, but it was applied extensively in the 2001 elections by both blocs.

The basic differences between the two systems cover the aspects of candidatures, threshold, unbundling procedure, proportional method, ballots, and connection between the two mechanisms of election:

- Independent candidates are allowed to stand for the Senate, but for the Chamber of Deputies, all candidates running for the single–member districts have to declare their affiliation to one or more lists running for the multi–member districts.
- The election of the Chamber of Deputies fixes a threshold for the allocation of the seats allocated with proportional rule.
- In the Senate all the votes received by the winning candidates elected with plurality rule are ignored in the allocation with the proportional rule.
- The Chamber of Deputies uses the Hare formula and the Senate uses the d'Hondt formula for allocating seats in the proportional tier.
- The voter receives two ballots for the Lower House, but only one for the Upper House. Consequently the list competition is much more evident and the voter can split her/his vote.
- The mechanism of election with proportional rule at the Upper House always produces a double representation of some districts, since the winners on the basis of the proportional rule come from the number of the candidates of the single–member districts. In the election of the Lower House this can happen only if the lists presented for the multi–member districts result are too short to fill all the seats won by any given party.

Some significant implications of the new electoral system

The principle of proportional representation allows each and every party to run alone as having specific and distinct traits is a resource in the electoral competition. Plurality systems in general discourage the creation of new parties and divisions in the old ones, the only exception being parties with a geographically concentrated electorate.

The new electoral law was a compromise between the pressure to lead Italy toward a bi–party system and the interest of parties to maintain their identity. The result was a mixture of incentives to aggregate parties and mechanisms of protection of smaller parties.

The relatively high number of seats awarded with plurality rule and the four–percent threshold nationwide favors the formation of alliances that will be part of the proportional allocation for the Lower House. On the other hand, the two ballots for the Lower House and the mechanism connecting the two votes spoil the aggregating pressure of the plurality rule for all those parties that are likely to pass the threshold. The disincentives to form electoral coalitions are threefold (D'Alimonte and Chiaramonte, 1995, pp. 48–49):

- The allocation with the Hare method of a single national district guarantees them as many seats as their electoral strength.
- The unbundling mechanism is applied to all the parties supporting the winning candidates of the single–member districts, proportionally to their vote shares in the proportional segment. This means when parties help a winning candidate belonging to a different party they reduce their chances of electing their own candidates in the proportional segment. Parties that support others' candidates will then claim some compensation for the possible loss.
- The candidates defeated in the majoritarian competition are added to all the lists they were affiliated to and will be elected if any of the lists are too short to fill all the seats they won. If the list is not affiliated to any candidate, candidates from the same list in another multi–member district with the best–unused remainders will be elected.

The disincentive of aggregation plays then at two levels: First, all the parties that can expect more than 4 percent of votes nationwide have no incentive to propose common lists for the multi–member districts. Second, each list has to evaluate the opportunity to support common candidates, considering the costs deriving from the unbundling and the compensation offered by the other partners.

Dynamics within the party system of the first and the second republics

The Italian party system of the so–called First Republic was characterized by very high stability (not of cabinets, though) that rather resembled immobility.

With the return to democracy, old parties returned to the government and new ones were founded. In the first election of the Republic (1948) the Christian Democrats (DC) gathered the widest support; they were followed by the Socialists and then the Communists.

The Communists (PCI) and the nostalgics of the neo–fascist Social Movement (MSI) were always excluded from every government coalition, while the DC were always in government, forming alliances with the Socialists (PSI) or Republicans (PRI), Social Democrats (PSDI), and Liberals (PLI).

The picture of the relevant actors in Italian politics remained virtually unchanged until 1987 when the Greens and the Lombard League entered the political arena by winning seats in the Chamber of Deputies and the Senate. Both the new actors were single–issue and somehow post–materialist parties (Aguilera de Prat, 1999, p. 16) and their success can, in retrospect, be interpreted as a first sign of voters' dealignment.

In 1989 the process of change within the party system became irreversible. Two factors are generally considered the most important causes to this change: the fall of the Berlin Wall and its effects on the left (see Morlino, 1997, p. 104; Donovan, 1995, p. 51) and the corruption scandals which involved almost all the parties, but particularly the DC and the Socialists.

The fall of the former Soviet Union and the process of German reunification weakened one of the traditional cleavages in Italian politics creating a favorable cultural and political environment for the modernization of the Communist Party. In February 1991 the PCI concluded its transition and changed its name to Democratic Party of the Left/*Partito Democratico della Sinistra* (PDS), while the more orthodox fringe created a splinter party with the name Newly Founded Communists/*Rifondazione Comunista* (PRC).

At first impact the new image of the party did not seem particularly successful since it was still unable to challenge the diarchy of the DC and the Socialists. These obstacles were wiped away in 1992—1993 by the corruption investigations. The PDS survived the first years of *Tangentopoli* ("bribesville") without being involved. In addition, its support increased thanks to its position in favor of the reforms movement.

In the 1989 European election Umberto Bossi, the leader of the Lombard League, managed to gather several northern regionalist movements under the symbol of the Northern League/*Lega Nord* achieving brilliant success, which was repeated in the 1991 regional elections. The Northern League was able to mobilize mass electoral volatility and to channel this movement into a mass party (Donovan, 1995, p. 53). In particular, the Northern League was able to challenge and defeat the DC in the North–East, which was traditionally characterized by the DC subculture, and in 1992 and 1993 they overtook the Socialists in their stronghold of Milan.

The disintegration of the old party system set off a troubled season in the party domains. Attempts were made to restore the old power balances by all the scattered forces, but with varied results. Some former leaders disappeared into total oblivion, others were jailed, some fled the country, and some realigned by founding new parties or by joining new formations.

One of the effects of the decline of the DC was also the growing difficulty of keeping all the different streams within the party together. Since the summer of 1993, the DC had split into several pieces and on the eve of the 1994 general elections the Christian Democratic "diaspora" established the Italian Popular Party/*Partito Popolare Italiano* (PPI), the Christian Democratic Center/*Centro Cristiano Democratico* (CCD), the *Unione di Centro* (UdC), the *Cristiano Sociali*, and The Network/*La Rete*. In the following years some of these new formations would disappear and other parties were formed in response to the demands of the changing general political situation.

From the collapse of the Socialists the Democratic Alliance/*Alleanza Democratica* (AD) was formed, while many former socialists joined *Forza Italia*. In the late 1990s the troubled former PSI followers formed a series of tiny new parties: the *Nuovo PSI*, and the *Socialisti Democratici Italiani* (SDI).

The majoritarian constraints of the new electoral law obliged all these parties to "choose sides" as far as the electoral coalitions were concerned. Some joined the Pole (or House) of Freedoms led by Berlusconi, others the Center–Left Coalition of the *Progressisti* and later, the Olive Tree. In the precincts of the right, the most important change was initially the renovated image of the post–fascist Social Movement/*Movimento Sociale Italiano* (MSI) which changed its name to *Alleanza Nazionale* (AN) and espoused a more moderate ideology.

The event that by far epitomizes the change in the Italian political arena was the creation in January 1994 of *Forza Italia* by the media mogul Silvio Berlusconi. Advantaged by the enormous void in the political arena that the downfall of the traditional parties had brought about, he was clever enough to fill that empty space by *inventing* a brand new party. The fast growth of *Forza Italia*, which only four months after its foundation won the general elections, was explained by the massive and skilled use of televised political communication and opinion polls (see Mazzoleni, 1995). By using shrewd marketing techniques, Silvio Berlusconi was able to gain the passionate support of the orphans of the DC, the PSI, and of the other fractured parties of the center.

In general one could say that the parties that survived the shake–up of the early 1990s gained a rather strong position in the new party system. The PDS benefited in three ways: a new image, a very limited involvement with the scandals that destroyed the credibility and legitimacy of all the other traditional parties, and the vacuum remaining in the left after the collapse of the Socialist Party. The *Lega Nord* became one of the leaders of the crusade against the *Tangentopoli* scandals since they had always been opposed the traditional parties. *Forza Italia*, as a completely new party, could fill a gap in the electoral spectrum and could also claim to be introducing a new way of doing politics. Led by a successful entrepreneur and (at the time) not touched by judicial investigations, *Forza Italia* presented itself as closer to the needs of the voters, and particularly to the middle–class voters, orphans of the PSI and DC. The National Alliance left its marginal role to become one of the key actors of the Second Republic.

A glance at the list of parties in the Italian party system in the general elections of 1994, 1996, and 2001 suggests that their number remained rather high and in particular much too high in the competitive context of the new electoral system in spite of the common belief that the new electoral system would simplify the political arena. This apparent contradiction can be explained by the strategy adopted by all the parties to form alliances for the Senate and the single–member districts of the Chamber of

Deputies and to then run alone for the proportional segment of the same House. The structure of the alliances changed across the three elections run under the new rules, nonetheless, showing a tendency toward stabilization.

Party coalitions for the 1994 general elections

In 1994 three blocs were competing for the single–member districts: the center–left, represented by the *Progressisti*, the center, represented by the Pact for Italy/*Patto per l'Italia*, and the center–right represented by the Freedom/Good Government Pole.

The picture of the alliances was rather complex. On the one hand (unexpectedly) the parties of the center, trying to escape the two–party logic that was starting to take root in the electoral dynamic, ran alone, but with very limited success. On the other hand (following a strategy foreseen by many scholars), the center–right presented two different coalitions: one for the northern and center Italy (Freedom Pole) and one for the southern regions (Good Government Pole).

The leftist bloc of the *Progressisti* included the Democratic Party of the Left (PDS), the newly founded Communists, the Greens, the anti–mafia movement The Network (*La Rete*), some remainders of the Socialists, the left–wing of the former DC under the label of Social Christians, and a part of the former Republicans with the label of Democratic Alliance. The centrist core of the former DC, renamed the Italian Popular Party, and the party linked to the referendum movement (Segni Pact) formed the centrist bloc (see Mudambi et al., 2001; Vassallo, 1997; Di Virgilio, 1997; Ignazi, 1995).

The center–right was constituted by a core of parties allied nationwide, supported in northern Italy by the *Lega Nord* and in southern Italy by the National Alliance (AN). *Forza Italia*, the rightist wing of the ex–DC (Christian Democratic Center), the former Liberals (then Center Union [UDC]) and the Radicals/*Lista Sgarbi–Pannella* formed the stable core of the center–right.

Notwithstanding the mutual hostility between the AN and the Northern League, the geographical differentiation of the center–right proved electorally successful. The three major partners found a common denominator in opposition to communism and in the renovation of politics and by stressing these issues they minimised the risks of a division. The disagreement surfaced when the three partners had to govern together. After only eight months the Berlusconi cabinet had to resign because the *Lega Nord* slammed the door in the coalition's face.

Party coalitions for the 1996 general elections

In 1996, when the caretaker cabinet led by Lamberto Dini fell, new elections were held, after which the structure of the blocs was altered. The first big change was the disappearance of the centrist bloc. In 1995 the PPI split into two groups, one of which kept the old name and the other taking the name of United Christian Democrats (CDU). At the same time, most members of the Segni Pact joined the new party founded by Dini, Italian Renewal (RI). The Northern League decided to run alone. The center–right parties formed a national coalition under the symbol of the Freedom Pole.

In the center–left bloc, a brand new coalition under the name of the Olive Tree (*L'Ulivo*) was formed led by Romano Prodi. It included the PDS, the PPI, the Greens, and the RI. The far leftist Newly Founded Communists did not join the coalition but signed up a stand–down agreement concerning the candidates in a number of electoral districts.

The Olive Tree was not only meant to be an electoral cartel, but also a government coalition in case of victory. On the other hand, the stand–down agreement with the Newly Founded Communists was only in terms of the electoral phase, since this partner was not willing to share government responsibilities with the Olive Tree.

The center–right coalition, after losing the Northern League, consolidated around the two major parties, *Forza Italia* and the NA, with the additional support of two new heirs of the DC: the CCD and the CDU. Shortly before the election the center–right managed to conclude an agreement with the Radicals/*Lista Sgarbi–Pannella*, which nevertheless presented autonomous candidates for the Senate as well as for both tiers of the Chamber of Deputies.

It is important to note that for the Freedom Pole the presence of the NA in all regions shifted the center of the bloc to the right; the competition between Berlusconi and Fini to be premier in case of victory enhanced the image of division and limited the capacity to mobilize the electorate (Di Virgilio, 1998, p. 8). The Northern

League and other smaller parties were addressing similar target areas, stealing decisive votes in some highly competitive districts. There were harsh conflicts within the bloc due to diverging opinions on specific policies.

The center–left, on the other hand, managed the complexity of the many different factions and was able to include a number of small regionalist parties that were not aligned in any bloc in 1994. It was under these circumstances that the Olive Tree coalition won the elections and succeeded in governing for the entire legislative period, even though there were four different cabinets (led by Romano Prodi, Massimo D'Alema I, Massimo D'Alema II, and Giuliano Amato).

Party coalitions for the 2001 general elections

The strategies worked out by the parties on the eve of the parliamentary elections of 2001 were concentrated on the "Berlusconi factor" even more than the previous contests. The center–left coalition moved in three directions: the search for a leader who could stand the challenge of a strong man in the opposition front; to bring together the fragmented and quarrelsome parties of the bloc into a strong alliance; and to capitalize on the good performance of five years in government. Although he had no previous government experience, Francesco Rutelli, the popular mayor of Rome was chosen as front–runner to attain the first goal. The choice was symptomatic of how image, personal attributes, and media savvy are becoming crucial in the creation of political leadership in postmodern politics. Critics of this move suggested that an incumbent prime minister would have been better to beat a dangerous adversary such as Berlusconi. The strength of the alliance was reinforced by different actions, the most significant of which was the foundation of a new party, The Daisy (*Margherita*), that gathered the forces of the center of the center–left bloc: the Democrats/*I democratici*, Italian Renewal/ *Rinnovamento Italiano* and (especially) the Popular Party (PPI). Eventually the coalition, under the Olive Tree emblem was made up of *Democratici di Sinistra* (DS), The Daisy, Greens, and *Comunisti Italiani* (CI). The far–left party, Newly Founded Communists (PRC), did not join the coalition this time choosing to run alone.

On the opposite front Berlusconi attained a major political result when he succeeded in convincing the Northern League to join The House of Freedoms coalition. The other parties composing the center–right bloc were of course the leader's own personal party *Forza Italia*, National Alliance (AN), and the CCD–CDU union of tiny ex–DC fragments. The charismatic leadership of Silvio Berlusconi was the true bond that kept together an oddly assorted cluster of political platforms and interests. It was more a cartel than a coalition (Bartolini and D'Alimonte, 2002, p. 247). However, it was a very successful one looking at the outcome of the elections that secured an unprecedented overwhelming majority for Berlusconi in both Houses of the new Parliament and (supposedly) presented a strong mandate for his cabinet.

A party system unresolved between the majoritarian drift and the temptations of the proportional system

The outcome of the 2001 general election is still under close investigation by political scientists, as it appears to have been the (expected) confirmation of the benefit of the transition set off by the new electoral law that introduced the mixed PL—PR rule. The dominance of the winning coalition (with a majority of 107 seats in the Chamber of Deputies, and 42 seats in the Senate) in Parliament seems to have stabilized a bi–polar system, at the expense of the third–party ambitions of nostalgics of the old customs (Bartolini and D'Alimonte, 2002, p. 10).

Nevertheless, in relation to the inauguration of bi–polar competition and the production of clear numerical majorities, the new mixed system fails to overcome the fragmentation of party representation. On the contrary it makes it more severe by exalting the electoral weight and the blackmail potential of the minor parties. The new system also fails to guarantee the aspirations of the Italian electorate who voted massively for the change to the plurality rule in the 1993 referendum: the stability of cabinets. The new rule was worked out in such a way that it stimulates the formation of all but homogeneous coalitions (Melchionda, 2002, p. 31). The electoral reform was not followed by a parallel revision of the form of government, which applies the same patterns as the First Republic. The prime minister is not elected directly by the voters, but is the expression of the winning majority, and so is hostage to the many components of the coalition. In the face of a quite heterogeneous composition of forces, and a low level of intra–coalition cohesion, it is likely that sooner or later the alliance will become strained, as Di Virgilio insists: "in 1994 the winning electoral coalition broke after only seven months from the ballot; in 1996 it lasted longer, but after about two years it underwent a parliamentary 'transformation' that opened the way to the formation of three short–lived cabinets" (2002, p. 28).

If this evidence is well founded, as the 1994–2001 data and trends seem to show, the expectation that the new mixed PL–PR rule would reduce the fragmentation of the political spectrum yielded by the old proportionalism—with all its negative implications that had brought public opinion to demand a radical change of the system—remains largely unfulfilled. According to leading Italian political scientist Giovanni Sartori, the

> ill–famed proportional rule of the 1948–1993 period had given birth to five–six significant parties, while the new law has generated three times as many parties. . . . The prevailing explanation is that the proliferation of the tiny parties is triggered by the proportional quota of the law. This is wrong. The truth is that the "too–many–parties" have been generated just by the plurality quota and by the "blackmail power" that the single–member districts give to the small parties (2002, p. 110).

To the "structural" reasons brought forward by Sartori should also be added the inveterate practices of the Italian parties still tied to the old proportional patterns and habits. One is the "proportionalization of the plurality rule," that is, the strategy of the parties to form "electoral cartels" based on clever agreements of the partitioning of candidatures in the single–member districts (Bartolini and D'Alimonte, 1995, p. 319). Another typical practice is to unite before the elections and to split afterwards. Thus, if fragmentation is avoided during the campaign it readily comes back in Parliament where the small parties, entitled to substantial individual financing, tend to distinguish themselves from the coalition and form their own independent groups (Pasquino, 2002, Dall'Ulivo... p. 86).

It is of great interest to note that in the summer of 2002 Parliament voted in a bill that ingeniously increases the amount of reimbursements for electoral expenses paid by the State Treasury to political parties. A 1999 amendment of a 1993 law had fixed the *una tantum* contribution to €0.415 for each vote obtained in the general election, provided that the party had reached the four–percent threshold, or 1 percent of the vote with at least one elected MP in one single–member district. The new law generously looks after the needs of all parties that have reached at least 1 percent, even if no candidate is ever elected. The pro–capita allowance grows by €1.00 each year of the legislature, with a net increase of 968 percent. No matter how strong the public indignation in the media, the decision by all parties represented in Parliament reveals perhaps more clearly than any other systemic indicator how durable are the "proportionalist inclinations" in the country's party system. If the four–percent threshold is formally maintained in the electoral mechanics, it is ultimately made void in the practical working of the political machine. Angelo Panebianco, political scientist and commentator for the leading Italian daily *Il Corriere della Sera*, in a critical editorial in the same newspaper observed:

> The public funding of the parties was formally abolished in 1993 by a referendum. Now it is resurrected and extended, retro–actively, even to the mini–groups that lost the elections, thus guaranteeing for the future the fragmentation of representation and the survival of party micro–bureaucracies, fed by tax–payers' money (14 July 2002).

To be sure, most parties profess their allegiance to the new prevalent plurality system. However they do not demonstrate enough "training" in its practice, and even fear its effects (Cotta, 2002, p. 30). Yet, the results of the 2001 elections prove that the new PL–PR system has begun to function because the political forces have themselves started to adjust to the constraints: the electorate, in fact, rewarded the parties that demonstrated their ability to pursue a bi–polar strategy and punished any third–force attempt (Cotta, p. 38).

The pro–majoritarian outlook of the Italian electorate that does not reveal signs of weariness after three elections with the new rule (not to mention the several other elections: European, city, regional, etc.) is perhaps the most significant difference from the German and New Zealand cases. After almost five decades of perfect (proportional) representation of their political divides, Italian voters have discovered the benefits of the plurality system and are getting used to it; thus, confirming Duverger's law of the gradual accustomisation to PL–based bi–polarism (Riker, 1982).

If this is the trend, what is the meaning of the proportional quota (25 percent) in the electoral dynamics? It becomes increasingly clear that it was introduced first to cater to the parties' interests and secondarily to allow a balanced representation of the people's will.

The bi–polarisation of the electoral results shows that Italian voters are realigning accordingly. "Most voters seem in fact to have developed a stronger identification with the coalition than with a single party. . . . One could speak of the vote for the PL quota in terms of an 'identity' vote or a 'vote of the heart'" (Natale, 2002, p. 311).

Is this choice of the Italian electorate to be considered a renunciation of representation of its many diverse identities? There is no easy answer to such a question. The evident erosion of party allegiance, the decline of political participation (proved by the dramatic multiplication of non–voters), the increasing search by voters for decisional shortcuts, and the personalization of political offerings are all factors underlying the majoritarian drift in the Italian electoral arena of the first post–Reform decade.

Part Two

Introduction: The Modernization of Election Campaign Practices

In Part One of this book we examined issues regarding the quality of representation of citizens in government. As long as we accept governance by representation we must have some means of selecting who it is that will best serve our particular interests and whom, therefore, we would be prepared to endorse as our representative. The role of representative is, of course, highly sought after as the office carries with it numerous perceived advantages; such as its degree of power and financial reward. For some, it will also mean the chance to shape public policy in such a way as to serve what is perceived to be the best interests of society. We choose our representatives through the democratic institution of election campaigns. It is within these campaigns that candidates seek to represent themselves to their voting publics with ever more sophisticated strategies. Representation of candidates to voters is the focus of Part Two where we examine the campaign features and strategies employed in Germany, New Zealand, and Italy. In examining the characteristics of election campaigns we also examine how those characteristics have been adapted to be effective within the context of the electoral system.

In order to discuss and compare the features of election campaign strategy in different countries it is useful to have some benchmark as a basis for that discussion. That benchmark has long been established as the "American" model, adopted to various degrees in democratic nations around the world through a process commonly referred to as Americanization. Because the model has evolved with the global development of technology such as television and because the sharing of campaign strategies has not been in a purely one–way flow from the United States, the extent to which "American" is a suitable label for the model is questionable. Mancini and Swanson (1996) are among those who have concluded that the term "modernization" is a more appropriate one for the process than is "Americanisation." More recently there has been a call for adoption of the term "professionalization" (see Holtz–Bacha, 2002). Modernization is the term we employ in our discussion here.

The factors that characterize the modernization of electoral politics include a tendency toward a personalisation of political campaigns whereby the campaign focus is on personalities rather than issues or whereby individuals conduct their own campaigns independently, or at least relatively so, of political parties; a reduction in the influence of political parties; the professional–ization of campaigning techniques brought about by the influence of advertising and public relations consultants who have an increasing degree of influence, not just in the formation of campaign advertising but in overall campaign strategy (Franklin, 1994; Wernick, 1991); and the structuring of campaign agendas around those of the mass media, particularly television (Blumler and Gurevitch, 1995; Franklin, 1994; Kavanagh, 1995; Mancini and Swanson, 1996; Scammell, 1995; Semetko et al., 1991).

Although a feature of campaigns worldwide, the personal–isation of political campaigns is particularly evident in those countries, such as the United States, where the electoral system concentrates on individual candidates. By contrast, in Western European countries and in New Zealand (among others), the political parties play the key role. The argument as to why these differences occur is cyclical: political parties are weakened when candidates use their own money and control their own campaigns while the fact that candidates campaign independently of political parties serves to weaken the power of the parties. In countries where power is retained by the parties, campaign funding is controlled by the parties.

The 1992 United States presidential campaign of Ross Perot, who used his private resources to run as an independent candidate, is an extreme example of a personalised campaign (see Lemert et al., 1996). When individual candidates do use their own resources to run their own individual campaigns it is often at the expense of the influence of political parties (Mazzoleni, 1996; Swanson and Mancini, 1996) because the candidate is less reliant upon the party for fundraising and organisational support. Generally, campaigns run under a first–past–the–post electoral system tend to be more personalised than those under systems of proportional representation (Mazzoleni, 1996) because voters place a vote for an individual rather than a political party, even though their choice may be driven by party loyalty. However, the ongoing importance of political parties at an organisational level and identification with parties as a basis for political loyalty should not be ignored (Mayhew, 1997). In many countries the centrality of political parties in the electoral process is not in dispute. Systems of proportional representation safeguard at least a degree of power for political parties as voters are required to place a vote for a party with those votes determining the number of successful candidates to be drawn from a party–selected list.

Modernization of the campaign process

In the Introduction to Part One we acknowledged the key role played by the mass media as an agent of representation by politicians and candidates to voters. The increasing dominance of television as a medium for reaching potential voters has clearly been a strong influence in the trend toward the personalisation of politics and political campaigns. The highly visual nature of television lends itself best to images rather than the detailed treatment of issues, which is better handled by the print media (Dahlgren, 1995). It also, importantly, has the capacity to deliver the subject, in this case the political candidate, directly and personally to the voter via the screen (Swanson and Mancini, 1996). From a democratic perspective television allows the political candidate or party to address the voter within the private sphere bypassing the open interactive arenas of the public sphere. Even though candidate control over "direct" encounters such as this can be said to be limited to advertising, commercial imperatives and priorities of the mass media serve to limit the depth of critical exposure of candidates that could facilitate informed choices by voters and to favour, instead, sensational stories that sell news to consumers. When media corporations provide direct or indirect endorsement of a political candidate or party the potential for objective campaign coverage becomes even more remote. At least it can be argued that direct and open endorsement allows readers and viewers to know where media interests lie. It is when media contend that journalistic norms of objectivity and integrity prevail and yet provide biased coverage of candidates in the guise of news that voters can be limited in their ability to obtain the necessary information from which to make decisions for themselves. It is, perhaps, ironic that even where such media bias is evident news coverage of candidates is deemed to be more believable than advertising.

In spite of the fact that candidates may spend many hours trying to make face–to–face contact personally with voters the scale of contact required for success, as well as the credibility factor, means that the media, regardless of issues of partisanship, dominate election campaigns. Given the importance of television in providing candidate exposure, campaign schedules are designed to ensure media–trained candidates are available for evening news broadcasts. Candidates' speeches are written with a view to delivering "sound bites" to news media, particularly television, as it is those short, memorable phrases that are likely to be chosen by editors for inclusion in news coverage (Franklin, 1994; Jones, 1995). Campaign events are staged with television in mind, providing visually appealing or otherwise visually significant links between politicians, their messages, and their voters. However, many of these apparently modern techniques of political campaigning were in use well before the introduction of television. Political candidates have long employed professional consultants in the structuring of their campaigns and in the construction of images and slogans to run highly personalised campaigns (Gitlin, 1991; Mayhew, 1997; Rosenbaum, 1997; Scammell, 1995).

Although the evidence of early professionalization of electoral campaigning is clear, it is also true that since the advent of television and more refined polling techniques, especially from the late 1970s, the degree of professionalization has increased enormously (Mayhew, 1997). Today there are specialists in public relations, advertising, opinion polling, direct mail, computer–isation, and media; consultants whose analytical techniques have become increasingly sophisticated (Levine, 1995; Semetko, 1991). As Wernick (1991) puts it, "promotion has been drawn into the heart of the [campaigning] process" (p. 135). Advertisers and public relations consultants are now involved at all stages of campaign strategy. Political marketers use data from opinion polls, focus groups, and demographic sciences that utilise sophisticated computer software to identify voter concerns and make sure that they are reflected in campaign messages. They also use focus groups to pre–test campaign messages to ensure that they are worded in a way that will engage target voters. By making such connections, or by finding the right "buttons" to push, the marketers facilitate the integration of issues from civil society into the political field in such a way that they will increase the appeal of their political clients. The ability of political candidates to generate mass appeal is arguably more important under majoritarian "winner–take–all" electoral systems where candidates must appeal to as many voters as possible if they are to have any role in government. Under proportional systems there is far more likelihood that candidates can enter government as a minor coalition partner.

If society is in crisis, equally divided on a key issue of national importance and consequently highly politically motivated, candidates can, and indeed must, make their stance on that issue the key focus of their campaign. Usually, however, that is not the case and the high stakes lead to the creation of catch–all parties that seek to occupy the central ground along with the perceived majority of public opinion and at the expense of minority opinion. With candidates all trying to appear to agree with the same groups of voters, personalisation is extended to issues, reducing campaigns to contests of image. The democratic implications of parties' clustering in the political centre and competing for the same votes are discussed in the Introduction to Part One.

Political advertising strategies

As stated earlier, political advertising provides the most reliable, although least credible, opportunity for candidates to represent themselves directly to voters. The degree to which campaigners can disseminate party or candidate messages through election advertising is clearly limited by the relevant legislation of different countries. In most West European countries political parties are not allowed to buy advertising time on television or radio but are instead allocated free advertising time that is used for broadcasting political advertisements. In New Zealand, parties work within strictly limited campaign spending allowances that can be used for buying advertising time and are also allocated airtime for political party broadcasts. At the other end of the spectrum, some countries, such as the United States, impose no limits on campaign spending. In most democratic countries, however, political advertising exists in some form, and global patterns have emerged. Well established, for example, is the technique of negative advertising which, although disliked by voters, is considered easier if not more effective than positive advertising (Ansolabehere and Iyengar, 1995; Diamond and Bates, 1992; Jamieson, 1992; Johnson–Cartee and Copeland, 1991; Maarek, 1995). The United States presidential campaign of 1988 is considered to have reached the peak of negative political advertising and is often the departure point for discussions of the implications of such advertising (see, for example, Jamieson, 1992; Lemert et al., 1996). The same campaign is also reported for the way in which the mass media amplified the negative advertisements by replaying them during newscasts, in many ways signifying the success of the advertising strategy in media manipulation (Jamieson, 1992; Kern, 1989; Lemert et al., 1996; Scammell, 1995). Once more, national variations apply: negative campaigning in Germany has only very recently begun to emerge as a trend, although it is directed at the party or program rather than at individual candidates.

Political television advertising as a genre facilitates a focus on images, although, image and issue concerns are clearly interrelated (Aden, 1989). Although "issues" are not and cannot be discussed extensively within a 15–or 20–second television spot, campaign strategists do sometimes use issue–oriented formats to support the image of a candidate (e.g., Rudd, 1986) and some studies have shown that issue formats can influence a candidate's image (e.g., Geiger and Reeves, 1991; Holtz–Bacha and Kaid, 1996; Kaid and Sanders, 1978). The personalisation of issues is often effected through the linking of a candidate to a personified entity such as crime (Kern, 1989). Levine (1995) maintains that "the most persuasive advertising in recent presidential elections [are] . . . ads that fuse together images and issues, using powerful symbols that enable voters to discern the different general policy orientations of the candidates" (p. 40). Levine also maintains that election critics focus on "the rise of the professionally mediated televised campaign" and fail to recognise that although "campaign strategists and advertising consultants continue to portray presidential candidates as embodying desirable personal leadership attributes" they also "utilise both personal image ads and more substantively based ads. Different appeals are used to reach different markets of voters" (Levine, 1995, p. 288).

Image development

Image is also an important precept for election campaigning. Prior to the development of campaign strategy, strategists decide upon an appropriate and marketable image and use it as a basis for the building of an identity of a candidate or party. Once decided upon, the "image is crafted through the media by emphasising certain personality traits of the candidate, as well as stressing various issues. . . . The outcome of this is the development of a 'position' for the candidate" (Newman, 1994, p. 12). Positioning of candidates, however, also needs to take account of the diversity of voting publics, a notion long understood by marketers and public relations practitioners and put to use with the targeting of messages tailored to specific audiences. This does not negate the principle of catch–all parties; it just means that the range of voters targeted by candidates can be broad and that one single image will not suffice. Like the individuals whose votes they seek, candidates must attempt to occupy multiple subject positions in order to maximize their identification with and self–representation to multiple publics. Levine (1995) observes that the United States presidential campaigns that they

> do not seek to present a single image of a candidate to the entire nation. Instead, campaign consultants use computer analyses of voter demographics in order to determine how a candidate will be marketed to different segments of the polity. Satellite hook–ups allow the candidate to "appear" before various groups of voters around the country, with messages tailored to each audience (p. 37).

Political marketers employ highly specialized computer demographic software to disseminate messages to various "market segments" through other means such as direct mail, telephone, and video distribution (Maarek, 1995; Newman, 1994; Scammell and Semetko, 1995). Tracking polls are undertaken at regular intervals to monitor campaign effectiveness and, in marginal constituencies, the development of voting preferences (Rosenbaum, 1997). Indeed, such polls are continued between campaign periods in what has been termed the permanent campaign (Scammell, 1995).

Equality of campaign discourse

Of particular concern to Bourdieu, and more broadly to democratic theory, is the unequal distribution of resources in the production of political campaign discourse. As modernization of campaign strategy further removes ordinary citizens from the politicians themselves, there is an increasing risk of public opinion being formed on the basis of misunderstood messages (Bourdieu, 1991). An unequal distribution of resources among political representatives can lead to the privileging of certain messages over others, a trend exacerbated in cases where the media fail to stick to their democratic role in the impartial dissemination of information. The political system, combined with the commercial imperatives of the media that result in a focus on media elites, can itself result in an unequal distribution of resources with minor parties being allocated less political broadcasting time and receiving less or no coverage in media reporting. Similarly, an unequal distribution of resources within social fields privileges particular individuals and groups in the accumulation of economic, cultural, and social capital. Capital accrued in social fields can be transferred to the political field as political capital in the form of direct influence in the production of public policy (for example) through substantial financial contributions to political parties to be repaid eventually with political favour. Capital in social fields (for example) through the agency of respected opinion leaders, can also be used to mobilize public opinion within the public sphere in order to influence public policy indirectly through the power of votes.

Habermas blamed the commercialization of the mass media and the concurrent upsurge in the practices of advertising and public relations for the demise of the public sphere where opinion on public policy should be formed independently of personal or economic influence. The features of the modern campaign certainly paint a bleak picture of the potential for election campaigns to provide the information necessary for such opinion formation, or for elections themselves to fulfill their fundamental democratic function. Nevertheless, the degree to which such practices can influence public participation in elections and at the elections' outcomes is further subject to constitutional, social, cultural, and historical variables within and between countries. For example, their success would also be affected, in part, by the caliber of the candidates, by the integrity of the media, and the degree to which they all seek to serve the public interest. Another key factor may be the electoral system itself, as explored in the following chapters.

Chapter Four

Germany: From Modern to Postmodern Campaign

There are different groups of factors that combine to make electoral campaigns in each country unique. Among them are certain background factors that are inherent to the political system, the socio–political context which usually only changes very gradually, and situational variables that can vary in the short term. In Germany the general frame is set by the constitution as it lays out the country's parliamentary system and explicitly assigns the parties a prominent role in it. The electoral system is largely defined in an electoral law, which could be modified compa–ratively easily but in fact has not been changed since the 1950s.

In addition to these laws only a few other regulations directly concern electoral campaigns. The length of the campaign is not fixed. The constitution dictates that parliamentary elections be held every four years. The election has to be held no earlier than 46 months and no later than 48 months after the beginning of a legislative period. This does not leave much leeway for the decision about the exact date, officially proclaimed by the German president. The only way to shorten the legislative period is by a vote of no–confidence, which can be held when it is thought that a chancellor has lost his majority in the parliament and a new chancellor candidate should be presented. The no–confidence vote, however, could also be instrumentalized by a chancellor who, for any reason, wants to open the way for earlier elections. This was indeed done twice under special circumstances, in 1972 and in 1982, but at once raised debates about the constitutionality of the procedure.

Thus, because the length of the legislative period is fixed, the parties can prepare their campaigns even before the exact election date is known. This actually gives them the opportunity to comply with the old strategists' wisdom stating that a campaign starts the day after the election. Whenever a campaign really starts, and in fact campaigns have become longer over the years, campaigning usually intensifies during the last four to six weeks before election day. This period is therefore called the "hot" campaign phase.

Equal opportunity for all parties has developed into the guiding principle for campaigning in Germany. Whenever the courts have had to resolve campaign–related conflicts, with several cases going right up to the Federal Constitutional Court, they have always made reference to this principle. However, equal opportunity in Germany usually is a graded equality, meaning that differences are made according to the "size" of a party as measured by the number of votes that a party receives at elections. The legal basis for this approach is found in *Article 5* of the German Party Law. It obliges all public institutions to treat parties equally, which refers to the use of public spaces (rooms, streets, and places), party financing, and the allocation of billboards as well as free advertising time on radio and television.

Since modern campaigning is very much dependent on the mass media and television in particular, the broadcasting laws deliver some further regulations for electoral campaigns. These laws mainly provide the framework for the parties' media campaigns targeted at the free media and for the advertising campaigns in the paid media.

Since the German political system, as laid down in the *Basic Law*, only provides at the national level for the federal government (*Bundestag*) to be directly elected by the people, these regulations apply to federal elections. Thus, the characteristics of the German electoral system, the two–vote system and the electoral thresholds (cf. Chapter One) can only have an influence, if at all, on *Bundestag* elections. Since most *Länder*, however, vote according to similar electoral systems, much of what applies to federal elections is also true at the *Länder* level.

Effects of the two–vote system:
Living on the second vote

Characteristic of the "German model" is each voter having two votes; the first given to a candidate in the constituency, the other to a party list. Having two votes allows for split–voting, meaning tactical considerations on the part of the individual voter. In addition, since one vote is given to a candidate whose name actually appears on the ballot, the system, although it attributes parties the decisive role, carries an element of personalization which the parties should take into account for their campaigning.

A major obstacle to the opportunities the parties have in this system, however, is the fact that a considerable share of the German voters does not understand the meaning of the two votes. One of the objectives of civic education and of electoral campaigning in general, therefore, is explaining the two–vote system to voters. Findings of polls have repeatedly shown that voters learn the meaning of the two votes during a campaign but soon forget again after the election. If parties build on the chances of tactical voting, and at least for the smaller parties there is good reason to, they have to explain the meaning of the first and the second vote to the voters or offer them simple instructions on how the votes should be used. The latter is done quite frequently in the parties' advertising with slogans like "The second vote is the vote for...."

The FDP has had a "second–vote strategy" since the 1960s due to the fact that the small parties only have a chance of winning a constituency and thus a direct mandate in some exceptional cases and because the FDP has repeatedly had to worry about not overcoming the five–percent hurdle. The second–vote strategy tries to maximize the share of second votes which actually determines a party's strength in parliament. The intensified efforts to gain second votes came along with various reasons in order to convince the voter. Because the FDP was the only other party between the two big parties for about 20 years, it presented itself as a third force necessary to prevent a two–party system and to avoid a single party government. As a result, it has always been in the interest of the FDP to make voters learn the meaning of the two votes and understand that they have a second vote they are supposed to give to the Liberals while they could use the first vote for the candidate of another party. As in this case, the second–vote strategy has frequently meant promoting a split–vote. Because the FDP's second–vote strategy and the vote–splitting that went along with it usually took place at the expense of one of the big parties, particularly its respective former or provisioned coalition partner, the term *Leihstimmen* (loaned or borrowed votes) was coined. A loaned vote means a voter gives their second vote to a small party in order to help it into the *Bundestag* although actually preferring another party. The international literature has offered the term "threshold insurance" for this strategy (Cox, 1997, p. 197).

Propagating itself as an indispensable third force has become a core element of the FDP's campaign efforts. Besides being repeated by candidates in their speeches and during their media appearances, the argument was often presented on posters and in the party's ads. The third–force argument was first brought forward during the 1965 campaign with slogans against a "black–red coalition" and "against a one–party rule . . . no matter if black or red" (Holtz–Bacha, 2000, p. 107). The election led to a coalition government of CDU/CSU and FDP. When the coalition broke a year later, the two big parties formed a grand coalition sending the small Liberal party into opposition. After the 1969 election, though, the FDP even lost votes compared to its 1965 result, but came back into government, for the first time as a coalition partner of the Social Democrats. During the campaign some party supporters promoted the idea of splitting the votes in order to help the FDP over the five–percent threshold. In fact, the FDP took the hurdle thanks to 1 percent more second than first votes (Roberts, 1988, p. 322).

When the Social–Liberal coalition lost their majority in the *Bundestag*, which was slim to begin with, due to defections to the Christian Democrats brought on by the government's *Ostpolitik* (détente with Eastern Europe), elections were called a year earlier after a deliberate vote of no–confidence. This time the FDP espoused an open second–vote strategy making it clear to SPD supporters that their party would not be able to stay in government without the Free Democrats because the SPD had never before succeeded in coming out from an election stronger than the CDU/CSU. The results of the 1972 election with a 3.6–percent difference between first and second votes proved the success of the FDP's second–vote strategy (Roberts, 1988, pp. 322–323). For the first time, the SPD came out of the election as the strongest party but was nevertheless dependent on the Liberals to form a government.

Because the FDP had also increased their share of votes compared to the previous election in 1969, the party felt strong enough to further stress its own identity in the 1976 election and even go for both votes. In addition to referring to the success of the Social–Liberal coalition, it pointed to its own role in the work of the government, particularly of its party leader and then Minister of Foreign Affairs, Hans–Dietrich Genscher, and made use of the old argument promoting the necessity of a third force (Holtz–Bacha, 2000, p. 121; Roberts, 1988, p. 323). In 1980, a highly polarized campaign worked to the advantage of the FDP, which for the second time in its history received a two–digit result. These elections were also the first time that the Christian Democrats nominated a politician from their Bavarian sister–party CSU, Franz Josef Strauß, as their chancellor candidate. His candidature, however, was disputed even among Christian Democrats. In addition to an anti–Strauß strategy, the Liberals again campaigned against a one–party government and maintained "It's do or die this time round"/"Diesmal geht's ums Ganze" (Holtz–Bacha, 2000, p. 125). Again the FDP openly engaged in a second–vote strategy. Since polls showed that many voters were prepared to split their votes in favor of the FDP, the SPD countered with their own second–vote strategy propagating that "the second vote is the vote for the chancellor"/"Zweitstimme ist Kanzlerstimme" (Roberts, 1988, p. 324).

After the change of the coalition in 1982, which took place without an election, the new Christian–Liberal government under Chancellor Helmut Kohl (CDU) paved the way for an early election in order to have his government legitimized by the electorate. The FDP, however, had all to fear from the election. After having left the Social–Liberal coalition, they had to fight the image of having betrayed Chancellor Helmut Schmidt (SPD). Several prominent politicians left the party and many of their voters also did not accept the political change caused by the FDP. During the campaign the Social Democrats tried to gain the sympathy of voters by playing up the betrayal of their former coalition partner. The FDP stressed the necessity of an independent third force ("Germany needs the Liberals") and again resorted to a second–vote strategy. With its new slogan "Liberty Needs Courage"/"Freiheit braucht Mut", the party adopted an ambiguous message delivering a programmatic assessment as well as justifying breaking up the Social–Liberal coalition and having made the political change possible. Convinced that an absolute majority was not possible for them, the CDU/CSU tolerated the second–vote strategy of the FDP which led to a 4.2–percent difference between first and second votes and thus proved to be extraordinarily successful (Holtz–Bacha, 2000, p. 128; Roberts, 1988, p. 322).

In 1983, the Greens made it into the *Bundestag* for the first time. In the long run, the FDP had to fear the new party as a competitor to its by now traditional and powerful role as a majority–maker for the two big parties. On the other side, the Social Democrats especially had to be wary of a new party on its left that might cost them second votes. For the 1987 *Bundestag* election, the FDP again incorporated the second–vote strategy in their advertising slogans. Since the third–force argument would have also been an argument in favor of the Greens, the FDP combined its efforts to attract second votes this time with programmatic statements pointing to what the Liberals stood for in their coalition with the Christian Democrats. At the same time, the FDP campaign also tried to raise fears of a red–green coalition and recommended itself as a necessary instrument against a single–party CDU/CSU govern-ment. Its campaign strategy was even more successful than in 1983. Not only did the FDP gain 4.4 percent more second than first votes, the party also increased their share of the vote by 2.1 percent to more than 9 percent (Roberts, 1988, pp. 322, 328).

At the time of the 1990 election, the first all–German election after unification, the political landscape had changed consider-ably. The extreme–right Republicans had achieved a certain success which had become visible at the 1989 European election. The PDS appeared on the scene, maintaining strong support in the East. The CDU/CSU, and even more so its Chancellor Kohl, who campaigned on his image as the "chancellor of German unity" and thus set the scene for a highly personalized campaign, enjoyed renewed popularity. The SPD and particularly its left–wing chancellor candidate Oskar Lafontaine criticized the costs of the unification process, which led to a campaign polarizing the two big parties. The FDP tried to jump on the bandwagon putting forward its party leader and Foreign Minister Hans–Dietrich Genscher and his role in the unification process. The second vote was declared to be a vote for Genscher. At the same time the party pointed to the possibility of an absolute majority of the Christian Democrats and its own indispensable role in preventing a one-party government. The FDP strategy proved to be right and the party gained an 11 percent share of the second votes. The (West German) Greens had instead tried to campaign against the patriotism coming along with unification by ambiguously stating "Without the Greens everything stays black, red and yellow," which are the colors associated with the three traditional parties, but also the colors of the German flag. By adopting this strategy the Greens misjudged the mood of the German electorate at the time and missed the five–percent threshold.

The good tidings for the FDP, as expressed in the share of second votes at the 1990 election, did not hold. In 1994, the party rang the alarm bells, warning simultaneously against a red–green and a grand coalition and trying to attract voters with the slogan "This time everything is at stake"/"Diesmal geht's um alles." The share of second votes for the FDP fell to 6.9 percent. The CDU/CSU experienced their worst results since 1949. Thanks to an unusually high number of surplus mandates for the CDU, the Christian–Liberal coalition remained; however, only with a small majority.

Over the years, since the party had helped the Christian Democrats back into government in 1982, the FDP had bound itself closely to the conservatives. When the Green Party established itself in the political landscape, two blocs developed with the CDU/CSU and the FDP on the one side and the SPD and the Greens on the other. Campaign slogans warning against a red–green coalition made this division visible. The Greens had demonstrated their fitness to govern in their participation in *Länder* governments. The *Bundestag* election in 1998 finally made the red–green bloc strong enough to govern. The SPD came out as the strongest party for only the second time in its post–war history and the Greens received a higher share of votes than the FDP, thus providing the new Chancellor Gerhard Schröder (SPD) with a comfortable majority.

If the split votes are taken as an indicator, research shows that the FDP with its second–vote strategy usually lives on votes borrowed from their respective coalition partner. During the 1970s, the major part of the split voters who gave their second vote to the FDP voted for the SPD with their first vote; during the other years the FDP's second votes mostly came from split voters who gave their first vote to the CDU/CSU (Jesse, 1988). Two reasons can be offered to explain this phenomenon. Either these voters preferred a certain coalition or they wanted to prevent a single party government.

It is above all the FDP that has cultivated the second–vote strategy to its profit. The other small parties (at least the Greens), whose chances of winning a direct mandate are also not good, have not exploited the strategy in the same way. While in 1998 the difference between first and second votes for the FDP was 3.2 percent, it was 1.7 percent for the Greens and only 0.2 percent for the PDS. Being in the opposition since 1998 has brought along changed conditions for the FDP because a second–vote strategy at the cost of another opposition party will not work the same way as it does when campaigning as a member of a coalition government.

In any case, for the party that uses it for its election campaign, the second–vote strategy means a tightrope walk if it goes for borrowed votes. Campaigning against the party whose voters are supposed to lend their second votes to a small partner is risky because it might be regarded as unfair. Thus, a party campaigning for borrowed second votes will have trouble presenting itself with an independent identity which, however, is perhaps what its "own" voters expect.

Effects of the two–vote system: The role of the first vote

The second vote is what counts. However, the availability of two votes, with the first vote to be given to a candidate in the constituency, makes the proportional electoral system a personalized proportional system and is one of the defining characteristics of the "German model" (cf. Nohlen, 2000, p. 327).

Whether the two–vote system really makes sense is nevertheless controversial among researchers. Particularly because studies have repeatedly shown that many German voters do not understand the electoral system and the meaning of the two votes, the two–vote system has been called into question. Pleas have been made in favor of a simplification in the form of a one–vote system like that in effect for the first *Bundestag* election in 1949, or at least a change of terms, in which the current second vote would be called the first vote just to make it clear that this is the vote that is (more) important (cf. Jesse, 1988; Schoen, 2000, Eine oder...). Others instead argue that the two–vote system has proven its worth irrespective of the widespread ignorance of the system and that it meets the main requirements of an electoral system, which are representation, concentration, and participation

(Nohlen, 2000, pp. 325–326). In addition, the increasing numbers of split voters, that is people using the possibilities of two different votes whatever it means to them, may be another argument in favor of the two–vote system.

However, as long as two votes are available, the question is what are the consequences of the personalizing element of the German electoral system for campaigns? Does the first vote play any role for campaigning? In fact, findings from various studies, particularly research into split–voting, indicate that the candidates in the constituency are almost irrelevant for the voting decision. In most cases voters are unaware of the names of the candidates running for election in their district (Klingemann, 1970, p. 175). Even prominent candidates cannot be sure to win their constituency. This is why most candidates who run in a constituency also strive for a place on the party list to make sure they get a seat in the *Bundestag* even if they do not win a direct mandate.

The major part of the electorate still votes "homogeneously," casting the second vote for one party and the first vote for the candidate of the same party; thus, not making a difference between the two votes. It is party preference and not the constituency candidate that drives this kind of voting behavior. Even when voters split their votes, reasons other than the candidates influence their decision. The personal component of the two–vote system plays a minor role for split–voting (Hilmer and Schleyer, 2000, p. 193).

However, the outcome of the 1994 and the 1998 *Bundestag* elections, which produced a surprising number of surplus mandates, may point to an increasing importance of constituency campaigning. After the CDU/CSU had won 12 surplus mandates (of 16 altogether) in the 1994 election, the SPD gained 13 in 1998. The SPD in 1998 specifically worked to this end. One of the 10 departments of the *Kampa*, the SPD's main campaign headquarters, organised Offensive '98, targeting 32 constituencies selected for intensified campaigning. These 32 constituencies were mainly constituencies where in 1994 the CDU had won against the SPD with only a slight margin. The campaign in these constituencies was designed according to detailed findings from survey research and supported by appearances of high–ranking party representatives. Nevertheless, special efforts in constituency campaigning like these do not necessarily mean an increasing importance of the constituency candidate. On the contrary, the fact that prominent politicians were sent into the contested districts for campaign appearances rather underlines the "party effect" on the first vote.

The success of the PDS in winning a substantial number of direct mandates, which in 1994 even helped the party to enter the *Bundestag*, also provides for a new perspective on constituency campaigning. This is even more true because it seems to turn upside down the old wisdom that small parties have no chance of winning a constituency that is behind the FDP's second–vote strategy. A study that examined the motives for split–voting in the 1998 election indeed reveals a new "splitting–structure on the left side of the political spectrum," a red–red combination. People give their first vote to the PDS and vote SPD with their second vote. This is a special phenomenon in the East while the traditional splitting structure for the leftist parties in the West is red–green with the first vote going to the SPD (Hilmer and Schleyer, 2000, p. 194). In those cases where the PDS managed to win four direct mandates in 1994 as well as in 1998, its success was due to prominent candidates who ran in these constituencies.

Strategic or tactical voting as the parties promote in their advertising presupposes a rational and sophisticated voter. Not only has the poor knowledge of the voting system cast doubt upon the effectiveness of these advertising strategies, research has additionally shown that, if at all, only small parts of the electorate decide on whom to give the first and who the second vote in a way that corresponds to the thinking behind the second–vote strategy. Instead, advertising of this kind may even have a detrimental effect (Schoen, 2000, Appelle zu…).

Personalization in a proportional electoral system

Although the personal element of the German electoral system does not provide for much personalization in campaigning, personalization has nevertheless been much discussed as part of the professionalization process. This, however, refers more to the national level than to the constituencies. A parliamentary system that attributes the roles of the main actors to the parties does not necessarily prevent personalization in the sense that parties push individual candidates in their campaigning or individual politicians themselves try to work on their prominence and thrust the party into the background.

Irrespective of the question whether candidates more than issues influence the decisions of the voters, parties have good reason to build their campaign strategy on candidates rather than on issues. Changes in the socio–political context of campaigns— the keywords being modernization and unpredictable voter—and changes in the media system that have fostered commercialization force the political system to adapt to the new conditions. This adaptation process can be called professionalization. Among the strategies adopted to win the attention of the media, particularly television, and of the electorate is personalization because it allows for an easier and more attractive conveyance of abstract political matters, diversion from difficult or unpopular issues, and identification (cf. Holtz–Bacha, in press; Holtz–Bacha et al., 1998).

In Germany, personalization is preferentially used by the big parties. Their campaigns are tailored more and more to their chancellor candidates, one of whom is usually the incumbent chancellor. Research has repeatedly shown that the incumbent chancellor enjoys a bonus because whatever he does is regarded as newsworthy (e.g., Semetko and Schoenbach 1994, p. 132). This effect, which works to the disadvantage of the challenger, has been called chancellor bonus, *Kanzlerbonus*. In 1998, using a highly personalized campaign combined with his media talent, Gerhard Schröder not only succeeded in maintaining a television presence throughout the campaign but also got more television time than earlier SPD challengers to Helmut Kohl, the incumbent of 16 years. In addition, Schröder was much more favorably evaluated than Kohl (cf. Schneider et al., 1999; Caspari et al., 1999).

The prominent role that the chancellor candidates play in the campaign is further mirrored in the slogans that the big parties use to attract party votes. Although the chancellor candidates cannot be voted for, the big parties try to associate the second vote with the chancellor. Already in 1949, the CDU campaigned on the slogan "Germany votes for Adenauer"/"Deutschland wählt Adenauer," which the SPD countered with "Ollenhauer Instead of Adenauer"/"Statt Adenauer Ollenhauer." Obviously inspired by the Kennedy campaign one year earlier, the 1961 SPD campaign, which provoked first allusions to Americanization, was very much concentrated on Willy Brandt who ran at the national level for the first time and, being comparatively young, was contrasted with the "old man" Adenauer. The television spots for the SPD all featured the slogan "Ahead with Willy Brandt"/"Voran mit Willy Brandt." For the 1969 campaign, in which Kurt Georg Kiesinger was the popular incumbent, the CDU created its famous slogan "What matters is the Chancellor"/"Auf den Kanzler kommt es an." In 1976, after Helmut Schmidt had taken over the chancellorship from Brandt, the SPD asked voters "Go along with us: Vote for Schmidt"/"Zieht mit: Wählt Schmidt." To counter the second–vote strategy of the FDP, but without mentioning the name of its controversial chancellor candidate Franz Josef Strauß in the 1980 election, the CDU stated "The second vote is the vote for the chancellor"/"Zweitstimme ist Kanzlerstimme." While personalization was used at varying degrees for Helmut Kohl during the 16 years of his chancellorship, the CDU campaign in 1990 was highly personalized to exploit his image as the chancellor of German unity. Ads in the print media told readers "This chancellor has achieved more than any peace movement" and "This is the chancellor you can trust" and posters used the byline "Chancellor for Germany. CDU, Freedom, Prosperity, Safety"/"Kanzler für Deutschland. CDU, Freiheit, Wohlstand, Sicherheit." A remarkable piece of Kohl's 1994 image campaign was a large poster that showed him shaking hands in a crowd, but without any text, not even his name (Holtz–Bacha, 2000; Toman–Banke, 1996).

Electoral advertising on television can also be taken as an indicator for the degree of personalization of party messages. Content analyses of party ads from 1957, when spots were broadcast for the first time on television in Germany, until 1998 show varying degrees of personalization in general and for the chancellor candidates in particular. Over time there has been no linear trend to indicate that personalization has been increasing. In most campaigns, the chancellor candidates are highly visible. Being present, however, does not necessarily mean that they are also made a topic of the text, either in their self–presentation or in the text spoken by others. The degree of personalization therefore seems to be dependent on the candidate and on the political context of the campaign (Holtz–Bacha, 2000, pp. 186–191).

In order to exploit the positive effects of personalization, the smaller parties try to adopt a similar strategy by concentrating on their top candidate or a team of prominent politicians from their ranks. While the advertising of the Liberals usually highlighted several of their leading politicians, in most cases, the FDP government ministers, the party started a more concentrated personalization strategy with the "Genscher Era." During the long years when Hans–Dietrich Genscher, then Foreign Minister, was its party leader, the FDP tried to emphasize his achievements. Most prominent in the 1990 campaign, the FDP pointed to Genscher's role in the unification process and emphasized his East German origins. Several of the slogans used referred to Genscher: "Vote for Genscher. Vote for FDP"/"Genscher wählen. FDP wählen," "My second vote is the vote for Genscher"/"Meine Zweit–Stimme ist die Genscher–Stimme," and "The absolute majority for CDU/CSU would be the end of the Genscher era"/"Die absolute Mehrheit für die CDU/CSU wäre das Ende der Aera Genscher." In order to capitalize on media's interest, the FDP nominated a "chancellor candidate" for the first time in the 2002 election campaign since it is unrealistic to assume that the chancellor would come from one of the smaller coalition partners in a government.

Even the Greens have succumbed to the necessity of a personalized strategy. When they entered the political scene, as part of their image as an alternative to the established parties, it was their declared objective to avoid any personalization and instead put issues first. In order to keep individual politicians from becoming prominent, they even adopted a rotation principle for top positions. Over the years, however, the Greens had to come to terms with some of their politicians becoming more popular than others and taking on a more central role because the press referred to them in their reporting or asked them for interviews more often. The best example for this trend was the career of Joschka Fischer who became Minister of Foreign Affairs in the red–green government after the election in 1998 and also became the most popular politician in Germany. For the 1998 campaign, the Greens distributed posters with his portrait and alluded to Fischer, who is known for running intensively every day, in their television advertising by showing the legs of a jogger.

In 2002 the Greens openly declared several of their leading politicians as the top candidates for the campaign.

Consequences of the five–percent hurdle

Although the five–percent threshold has worked and only a few parties are represented in the *Bundestag*, it does not prevent small parties from trying their luck and running for election anyway. The number of parties registered with the Federal Electoral Officer has even risen over the years. In 1994 and in 1998 more than 30 parties joined the race. Small groups are encouraged to run for election by the German system of party financing. Regardless of whether a party makes it over the 5–percent threshold and into the parliament, every party officially registered receives public money provided it gets more than 0.5 percent of the votes. In addition, no matter what their electoral success, the parties are entitled to free airtime for advertising on the public broadcasting stations or can buy advertising time on the private channels. Thus, every party running in a campaign has the opportunity to present its program to the electorate on radio and television. While these regulations provide equal chances for all parties running, the five–percent clause nevertheless has certain hindering effects.

The Green Party's road into the *Bundestag* and its establishment in the political landscape is a good example to show that a new party's success depends on much more than just receiving 5 percent of the votes. Since the political system is very much dependent on the media in order to reach the electorate, of particular importance is how the media deal with the newcomer and whether they regard the activities of a new party as newsworthy. Although the five–percent hurdle of the electoral law does not apply to the media's political reporting in any way, studies have found that a virtual five–percent clause is at work in the media. A study on the 1980 election campaign found that the threshold seemed to influence television's reporting about the small parties going as far as not mentioning them at all. This was also true for the Greens (Langenbucher, 1983, p. 115) even though the party had already reached 3.2 percent of the votes in the first European election a year before. Interestingly, attention for the Greens changed with the outcome of pre–election polls. As long as the polls showed the Greens were strong enough to make it over the 5–percent hurdle, the party was at least mentioned on television from time to time. As soon as it became clear that they would not make it, television did not bother with the party any more (Langenbucher and Uekermann, 1985, p. 54). Another study on the 1980 election confirmed this finding for television and for the press as well (Buß et al., 1984, pp. 85, 90). While the Greens only reached 1.5 percent of the votes in 1980, they jumped the five–percent hurdle in 1983 when they gained 5.6 percent. However, even then the Greens and their issues encountered a media barrier. Although representation in the *Bundestag* (and by now in several *Länder* parliaments) helped the Greens to an increased media presence, their program still did not get adequate coverage as an extensive content analysis of the press showed. Correspondingly, resonance of the Green's issues in the electorate, indicated by the attribution of competence, was low (Knoche and Lindgens, 1990).

The 5–percent hurdle also worked with regard to participation of the Greens in discussion programs on television. From 1972 until 1987 the public television stations broadcast highly popular campaign debates shortly before election day. These debates were restricted to the leaders of the parties represented in the *Bundestag* at that time. Only in 1987 did the Greens have the chance to participate in the debate. In this discussion, the representative of the Greens displayed a comparatively aggressive debate strategy which seemed to have been forced upon her by attacks of the other participants (Schrott, 1990).

A second problem for small parties resulting from the 5–percent threshold is its effect on public opinion through the publication of polls. If polls are published, and no regulations restrict the publication of opinion polls prior to elections in Germany, and they show the strength of a party close to 5 percent, this can have a negative effect on their electoral chances. If voters get the impression that their preferred party or the party they wanted to vote for to support a certain coalition might not make it over the five–percent threshold, they might ponder whether they are about to waste their vote. Votes lost because of such deliberations may be the very ones that would have helped a party to take the 5–percent hurdle and enter the *Bundestag*. This effect therefore has also been called a guillotine effect (Reumann, 1983). Parties for whom the polls show a share of votes close to 5 percent therefore have a great interest in appearing strong and optimistic about their chances on election day. The campaigning of the small parties in some earlier elections seems to show that they try to fight the guillotine effect by overstating their strength (Schmitt–Beck, 1993, p. 404; 1996, p. 142). In the 2002 election campaign, the FDP declared early on an electoral objective of 18 percent although they only reached 6.2 percent four years before. Research showing that voters prefer to give their votes to a party for whom entry into parliament is sure confirms the positive effect of such purposive optimism as part of a party's campaign strategy (Schoen, 2000, Appelle zu...).

Coalitions as a campaign issue

Even though the big parties, the CDU/CSU and SPD, have dominated the party structure since the 1950s, Germany has never really had a two–party system. With the exception of 1957 when the CDU/CSU reached an absolute majority, the strongest party after an election has always needed a coalition partner to attain a majority in the *Bundestag* and to get its top candidate elected chancellor. Since the establishment of the Greens during the 1980s and the appearance of the PDS upon unification, there are now five parties represented in the parliament. In other words, Germany has developed into a multi–party system. The chances of one party gaining an absolute majority have thus diminished. Coalition governments of two parties are the rule.

Future coalitions, therefore, are also a campaign issue. Parties have to decide in advance whether they will enter the campaign with a clear coalition commitment. Telling the voter whom the party wants to form a coalition with after the election may be in the interest of the second–vote strategy if a party is attempting to attract votes as threshold insurance at the expense of the coalition party. On the other hand, a firm advance commitment to one coalition may rob the party of the opportunity to keep its post–electoral options open for negotiations with both sides.

Possible future coalitions are also a topic for negative advertising. Warning against a grand coalition has been a repeatedly used strategy of the FDP, recommending itself as a necessary third force. Since other parties have entered the scene and made new coalition constellations at least theoretically possible, warning against red–green or red–red coalitions has become a recurrent campaign feature of the Christian–Liberal bloc.

Famous for this kind of negative strategy has become the so-called Red–Socks Campaign against the PDS in 1994. The CDU used a poster showing a red sock pinned to a clothesline and the slogan "Into the future . . . but not on red socks"/"Auf in die Zukunft . . . aber nicht auf roten Socken" right after the state elections in Saxony–Anhalt where an SPD–Green minority government had been formed. The PDS indicated they would support the red–green coalition but no formal coalition agreement was signed. Shortly afterwards the CDU came up with the slogan "Future Prospects, Not A Left Front. Safely into the Future. CDU"/"Zukunft statt Linksfront. Sicher in die Zukunft. CDU" for Saxony–Anhalt. At about the same time, the Red–Socks poster appeared but it was no longer used for the federal election campaign because of protests that came particularly from the East German *Länder*. Nevertheless, because of its simple but clear message, the poster became well known all over the country. In the 1998 election the CDU adopted a polarization strategy and tried a follow–up to the Red–Socks argument with the "Red–Hands–Campaign." A poster showed a handshake of two red hands, alluding to the forced merging of the SPD and the German Communist Party (KPD) into the SED in East Germany in 1946. The text accompanying the picture was the 1998 SPD slogan "We are ready. SPD"/"Wir sind bereit," adding PDS and the warning "Watch Out, Germany!"/"Aufpassen Deutschland!" This poster was controversial even within the CDU and it soon disappeared again (Holtz–Bacha, 2000, p. 146).

Also during the 1998 campaign the FDP warned not only against a red–green coalition but also supported the CDU's anti-PDS strategy by showing graffiti–style posters with the slogan "Red–Green + PDS" supplemented by "Us or Them, Second Vote for the FDP"/"Wir oder die. Zweitstimme FDP." In a similar way, another poster showing a smashed red tomato said: "Liberal or Red–Green–PDS. Second Vote for FDP." On the other side, the Greens recommended themselves as the only possibility for change: "Change is Green"/"Grün ist der Wechsel" and "New Majorities Only with Us"/"Neue Mehrheiten nur mit uns." In a more direct fashion, adopting the line formerly used by the FDP, the Greens pleaded "Vote Green Against the Grand Coalition"/"Wähl grün gegen die grosse Koalition," but also turned against the CDU with the statement "Without Green, Things will Look Black for You"/"Ohne grün sehen Sie schwarz" (Holtz–Bacha, 2000, pp. 146–147).

The prominence of the issue is confirmed by findings of a content analysis of electoral advertising on television. Statements referring to the election, which included discussions of future coalitions, explanations of the electoral system, the style of the campaign, and direct appeals to go voting, came out as the most important topic. In all campaigns since 1957, except of 1969, this topic ranked first. Among the electoral references, the discussion of coalitions reached its highest value in 1983 when the FDP had to defend their switch from the Social–Liberal to a Christian–Liberal coalition (Holtz–Bacha, 2000, pp. 176–177). However, the fact that coalitions are usually necessary in Germany makes campaigning on the issue a delicate matter. It is particularly difficult to campaign against the coalition partner of the last legislative period or against the possible future partner if a firm coalition commitment has been made. Attacking the former coalition partner might be regarded as a kind of betrayal and casts doubts on the party's own role in the coalition. This was the FDP's problem in the 1983 election campaign after it had switched from a coalition with the SPD to a coalition with the CDU/CSU. The FDP countered by trying to underline its courage in having made a necessary political change possible. Further, if one party attacks another during the campaign and then forms a coalition with that party after the election, they may end up with credibility prob-lems. In a way, the SPD was in this situation in 1998. Although a red–green coalition was the probable future constellation, the SPD had to distance itself from its possible future partner when some Green politicians came up with the (unpopular) proposal of an enormous hike in the price for petrol or the (equally unpopular) idea of limiting the number of flights per person for ecological reasons, both gloatingly exploited by the Christian Democrats and the Liberals.

The electoral system and the Party Law

The German Party Law, first passed in 1967, supplements the framework for election campaigns as set out by the electoral system. Extrapolating from the constitution, which explicitly stresses the role parties play in the formation of the political will of the people and their intermediary function between the state and society, the Party Law describes the role of the parties and their internal organization in more detail. Of particular interest for campaigning are the regulations of the Party Law with regards to party financing and equal treatment of parties. The dependence of much of the parties' financing on the number of votes they reach in an election has already been mentioned above. As a consequence, smaller parties of which cannot compensate for this difference through donations and the matching, state funds, have to live on considerably less money in an election campaign than their big competitors. As a result, a major challenge for the small parties is reaching the attention of the electorate among the overwhelming campaign efforts of the big parties.

The equal opportunity regulation of the Party Law refers to services provided to the parties by public institutions. The same article allows for graded allocation according to the strength of a party measured by the votes it received in recent elections. In addition, it determines that all parties represented in parliament and who are eligible for official party status, referred to as constituting a "fraction" (which is the case when a party has reached at least 5 percent of all seats in the parliament), have to be accorded at least half of the amount that other parties get. This regulation is applied to the number of slots the parties get for their advertising in public radio and on television. The broadcasting laws oblige the two public broadcasting stations to give free air-time to all parties registered for an election. Electoral advertising on television and the allocation system in particular have been the subject of several cases brought to the Federal Constitutional Court which, however, approved the graded allocation with smaller parties getting less time (fewer spots) than the larger ones. To allow for a certain repetition effect, the minimum number of television spots per party was set at two (per channel).

During the recent campaigns, with more than 20 parties running for election, CDU and SPD each received eight time slots on the two public television channels, 16 altogether. The smaller parties that are represented in the *Bundestag* got four whereas the smallest groups were allotted the minimum quantity of two slots. The maximum length for the individual spot to be broadcast during these slots in 1998 was 90 seconds. All parties can purchase additional time on commercial television where they have to pay the prime costs. In 1994 this was interpreted as 55 to 60 percent of the usual spot prices and 45 percent in 1998. As the campaigns since 1990 have shown, only the bigger parties can afford to buy advertising time on the commercial channels in addition to the free time they receive on public television. In 1998, of the six parties represented in the German national parliament only four purchased broadcasting time on the commercial television channels. Thus, even more than the graded system of free time allocation, the opportunity to buy additional time on commercial channels has undermined the equal opportunity rule that guided electoral advertising on television for a long time.

Conclusion

Although Germany's proportional voting system provides better chances for smaller parties than a majority system, smaller parties encounter some disadvantages in their election campaign. On the one hand, this is simply due to their size and their share of votes. Small parties have fewer members whom they can mobilize for their campaigning and they have less money to spend for their campaign because a great part of party financing is dependent on the number of votes that a party receives. The 5–percent threshold, which is a hurdle for small parties, is also effective in the attention of the mass media.

On the other hand, certain disadvantages result from the interpretation of the equal opportunity principle, which means graded allocation of services by public institutions, for instance, free air time for electoral advertising on public television and in radio. In addition, since all parties other than CDU/CSU and SPD have no chance of getting their candidate elected chancellor, smaller–party candidates are overshadowed somewhat by the chancellor candidates of the two big parties. This became most obvious when the FDP named a "chancellor candidate" for the election campaign in 2002. He tried to sue his way onto the television debate which, for the first time in German campaign history, was a duel between the two chancellor candidates.

To compensate for these disadvantages, the small parties have to find ways of campaigning that secure the attention of the mass media despite the overwhelming presence of the two big parties. This is a question of timing as much as of attention–seeking actions. Again the FDP can serve as an example here. In addition to naming a chancellor candidate the party led an "18 percent campaign" in 2002. Although the FDP have not often reached two–digit results, they claimed 18 percent to be their objective this time. The 18 appeared wherever an FDP candidate made her/his appearance, even on the soles of their shoes or on the collar of their shirts. One of their candidates is known for parachuting to his campaign appearances, thus providing for interesting pictures for television.

The small parties have also tried to make the best of their position as minor players in the party system. It is one of the constants of their campaigning to warn against an overwhelming or even absolute majority of one of the big parties or a grand coalition of the two. These arguments are also used when the small parties campaign for the second vote and thus try to pick the fruit over the fence of their coalition partners, not much to the amusement of the latter. However, coalition governments, which are the rule in Germany, prevent former or potential coalition partners from becoming (too) negative.

Chapter Five

New Zealand: Adapting to Proportional Representation

One of the key observations made in this book and elsewhere regarding election campaigns is that ultimately they are shaped by the unique social, historical, and political context of the countries in which they are situated. New Zealand has adopted the German model of proportional representation and its election campaigns certainly reflect many similarities to those run in Germany, yet they also bear their own idiosyncrasies. As outlined in Chapter Two, the political field in New Zealand is currently clearly divided along a left to right spectrum, although special issues, particularly that of genetic modification, also feature strongly. New Zealand's election campaign strategies also reflect the rapidity with which both its social context and its political system have changed.

For New Zealand, the change to a proportional from a majoritarian system has meant changes in the ways people vote for their representatives. Voters now have two votes; one for their electorate (or constituency) candidate and one for their preferred political party, and there does not need to be any consistency between them. Electorate candidates are chosen by the old majoritarian system—the candidate with the most votes wins the position and the rest of the electorate votes count for nothing. The party vote is the more important one for political parties as this is the vote that determines proportionality in Parliament, with numbers of Members of Parliament (MPs) being supplemented as necessary from party lists. Parties must win at least 5 percent of the party vote before entering Parliament at all, unless they win an electorate seat, in which case their party vote does not need to meet the 5–percent threshold. In this way, just one electorate (or constituency) seat can lead to the election of several other candidates from that party's list.

New Zealand political parties, as well as voters, have clearly had difficulties in adjusting their campaigning to the much more complicated new electoral system. These difficulties were apparent during the 1996 general election campaign period. Readjustments were made for the 1999 campaigns, although many of these were tentative and experimental. In 2002, further problems arose for political parties leading up to the election, suggesting that voters and politicians alike are still coming to terms with proportional representation, although continuously changing social factors that are external to the electoral system clearly also play a part in the need for ongoing revision of campaign strategy.

When proportionality became a reality in 1996, voters expressed concern about post–election coalition formation and about which party policies would be sacrificed in the formation of coalition agreements. As described in Chapter Two, voters' understanding of how the system worked and, in particular, of how each of their two votes could be influential, was low in 1996, even lower in 1999, and still not improved in 2002. Voters' lack of understanding of the overriding importance of the party vote has been reflected in the ways in which they attempt to influence the outcome of the election by voting tactically, very often giving their constituency vote to the party of their choice and the party vote to their preferred coalition partner for that party.

For political parties the key problems have been in having to campaign under new rules as well as having to contend with (or take advantage of) voters lack of understanding of the system. Many features of the three MMP election campaigns of 1996, 1999, and 2002 echo those of election campaigns around the world. However, changes have had to be made as well, although many of these have evolved as understanding of the new game has grown. What is evident are the new blend of campaign practices and tactics still emerging.

Campaign professionalization

The evolution of election campaigning in New Zealand, both under first–past–the–post and under MMP, has most notably been marked by a steady increase in the degree of their profession–alization. In this observation is included the use of campaign professionals in the design of campaign messages, the use of technology (especially in market research), and the sharing of expertise with international campaign managers. A further factor of the professionalization of election campaigns is an increased focus on disseminating campaign messages via the mass media, especially television. None of these features are new to New Zealand but, as elsewhere, they are tailored to suit the peculiarities of the New Zealand context.

Most of New Zealand's successful political parties share expertise with their counterparts overseas, although the degree to which they do so is dependent upon party resources and connections. A limitation to their use of international professionals that has been noted by campaign managers is the fact that most of those professionals, coming from North America, Australia or Britain, have expertise in campaigning under first–past–the–post electoral systems but not proportional ones. That limitation has meant that New Zealand strategists have had to make their own adaptations to campaign strategies and associated messages to suit both the local social context and the electoral system.

The National Party provides a clear example of international cooperation with its central strategic committee receiving and sharing strategy information with other parties of an international organization of center–right political parties, the International Democratic Union. As the manager of National's 1996 campaign explained:

> We had the opportunity because we had relationships with other center–right parties around the world to actually use those people and to get feed back and use them as a resource. We have that tie in [with the Australian Liberal Party] just as we have for the Republicans in the States and the Conservatives in the UK. We all belong to an organization of International Democratic Union and we can feed resources from those people in terms of our campaigns (personal communication, March 9, 1996).

Labour, too, uses campaign consultants from outside New Zealand, most obviously taking advice from Britain's New Labour Party officials and advertising people. Their influence was overt in Labour's adoption of Third Way politics and of a campaign blueprint that was first put forward by Clinton in the United States and then by Blair in Britain, as described below. In 1999, New Zealand's Labour Party adopted the British New Labour Party's very successful campaign tactic of a card of pledges, distributed to all households, which clearly stated leader, Helen Clark's, seven "commitments" for a Labour Government. The pledge card tactic was so successful that Labour repeated it in 2002, although this time the seven pledges were promoted as the "next steps," reflecting Labour's position as the incumbent party.

As elsewhere in the world, technology, particularly in the form of demographic computer software, is used to advantage in New Zealand election campaigns. In 1996 the National Party claimed that the computer technology available to them was second to none internationally. With the software, they identified key target groups and used them to disseminate messages designed to resonate within each group. In 2002, the Greens used the same technology, guided by an experienced American strategist, to successfully identify their own specific target and to run a carefully targeted campaign geared toward mobilizing support for their key issues.

Although advice is brought in from elsewhere, when it comes to running the campaign most New Zealand parties form their own campaign teams. These teams include, as far as financial resources allow, communication professionals but they also include party members. This has certainly been so for the National party whose strategic committee, the ultimate authority of the campaign team, is made up of key members of the National Party as well as its political wing. Although the use of technological expertise is consistent with international trends of campaign modernization, the high degree of involvement and influence of political party members is notably in contrast to the trend noted in the United States of a significant reduction of party influence in favor of individually run campaigns (Nimmo, 1996; Shea, 1996). National's campaign manager explained that

> we're very mindful in National that the party input is there, that it's not dictated to by the politicians – it's dictated to and has a greater influence by the consultative process that we have within the Party. The Party can feel assured that these things aren't going to be hoisted on them without the party's input and the party's signing off on them (personal communication, March 9, 1996).

There is tension, however, between the need for increased professionalization of campaigns and the desire for Party involvement through individuals who may be less adaptable than contracted consultants. Strategic adaptability has certainly been a requirement of successful campaigns in the changing political environment of New Zealand. As a former National Party MP stated:

> MMP has turned elections into battles of strategy. A party without a strategy will not be able to produce an MMP electoral result that puts them into government. Under the previous system of first–past–the–post . . . it was possible to win an election by making a series of tactical wins in electorates (Young, 2000, p. 30).

Campaigning for the party vote

As stated earlier, New Zealand voters, like their German counterparts, have had a poor understanding of the relative importance of their two votes since the introduction of proportional representation in 1996. Although this has clearly posed a problem for voters from the perspective of getting the government they thought they were voting for, it has also created a problem for political parties. Campaign messages had to be adapted to attempt to educate voters as well as to take advantage of the two votes, as appropriate. However, for some parties, what was appropriate in terms of the party's interest was not initially clear. Some political parties understood very well how they must adapt to the new electoral system while others did not.

As a minor party, the Alliance is reliant upon the party vote to enter Parliament, yet in 1996 it focused its campaign on the electorate vote. The party ran what was essentially a first–past–the–post campaign with an emphasis on door knocking by local electoral candidates. At the time, the campaign manager believed that if they were successful in obtaining electorate votes, party votes would naturally follow (Kirk, 1996), although after the election he admitted that this had been a mistake and that they should have campaigned more specifically for the party vote (Hubbard, 1996).

By contrast, Act, also a minor party but at the opposite end of the political spectrum from the Alliance, not only campaigned primarily for the party vote but understood the potential of split–voting to work in its favor. Act told voters that the first–past–the–post system had been undemocratic, ironic given the prominent role of key Act personnel in campaigning against the introduction of proportional representation (see Chapter Two). The strategy behind the assertion, however, was to promote the notion that a coalition government was desirable and could be assured by preventing National, Act's natural coalition partner, from being able to form a government (even a minority government) on its own. Act, who hoped to win National's party votes, accused National of giving its supporters "false information about how to vote tactically in an MMP election" (Act press release, 30 September 1996) and stated that "seeking party votes at Act's expense is a futile, expensive exercise in political vanity when the price is opposition for National" (Act press release, 29 September 1996). Such statements not only added to, but also took advantage of, voter confusion.

By 1999 it was evident that most party campaign strategists had adapted to the new electoral environment. The Alliance, along with the other minor parties, focused on the party vote. However, it also became evident that when small parties decide to campaign only for the party vote, even if they do stand nominal candidates for electorate seats, it can create difficulties for the larger parties who campaign for both votes. This is because the electorate candidates of the larger parties tend to be better known. In such cases, voters tend to give their electorate vote to one of the two larger parties and their party vote to a minor party. Reasons for doing so appear to be at least two–fold: it can be because of a misguided sense of fairness or as stated above, because, many voters believe that the two votes are of equal value. Voter concern about coalition arrangements, fueled by media speculation, is also likely to be a factor, with voters trying to help a smaller though less preferred party into power.

Campaign strategies and tactics, however, have not consistently demonstrated the benefits of experience. In 2002 the National Party was widely criticized, including among its own members, for failing to campaign for the party vote and allowing electorate candidates to pursue the electorate vote only. Their billboards frequently portrayed a local candidate asking for the electorate vote; this in contrast to Labour's that asked for either both votes or the party vote. National's decision to advertise in this way was surprising, especially in light of the lessons learned in the previous two MMP campaigns. Some commentators, including a defeated National list candidate, blamed the party's controversial president while others stated that the tactic was instigated by the party's political leader, Bill English, in order to "reconnect" with communities as part of an image–building campaign (Young, 2002). Whatever the party's reason, their failure to adequately campaign for the party vote has been cited as one factor in the worst election defeat ever suffered by the party.

Inter–party cooperation

The issue of split–voting is further complicated by the electoral system's waiver of the need to cross the 5–percent party vote threshold in cases where parties gain at least one electorate seat. For minor parties, this offers an opportunity to have several candidates elected on the strength of a locally well–known and popular individual. In formulating campaign strategies under MMP, minor parties have to calculate their chances in particular electorates, sometimes known as "trigger electorates," in order to determine whether or not they are worth the diversion of resources that would otherwise be put toward maximizing the party vote. Major parties need to calculate whether or not they should actively support electoral candidates of minor parties in trigger electorates, in the expectation that those parties will serve as coalition partners in government.

In 1996, National agreed not to run a candidate in one electorate that was being contested by a very popular local candidate, the leader of the United Party, who would cooperate with National in government. Act tried to pressure National to do the same for them when it eventually became apparent that their leader, Richard Prebble, could win the Wellington Central electorate. Although National needed the support of Act to form a center–right coalition, standing down its own candidate was not considered to be a viable option because of the already existing tension between the party and its electorate candidates. When National did tacitly endorse the Act candidate only the day before the election by publicly predicting his victory, the National candidate's feelings of betrayal were widely covered by the press.

Ideologically, Labour has always been the natural coalition partner for the Alliance, yet in 1996 the Alliance consistently campaigned aggressively and negatively against Labour. At the same time the Alliance took a non–negotiable stance on the need to enter coalition negotiations prior to, rather than after, the election. No other party was prepared to enter pre–election negotiations because they wanted to negotiate on the basis of a known power differential (the relative number of votes) that could only be determined by the election outcome. Those two strategies of the Alliance appeared to leave virtually no room for the two parties to work together in government. Furthermore, the messages that the strategies communicated were confusing for voters, exacerbated by the media's preoccupation with speculation regarding post–election coalition formation.

It was clear that voters were looking for stability in government and the Alliance's position could not have instilled voters with confidence that this was possible under an Alliance/Labour coalition. The way their position was communicated also suggested to voters that a vote for the Alliance would be wasted as the party had effectively ruled itself out of being a part of a coalition government. Labour and Alliance opponents, particularly National, added to the confusion with a strongly negative campaign that predicted instability with a center–left coalition. The key message of that campaign was that Labour, New Zealand First, and the Alliance would form a "high risk, unstable left–wing coalition." National's television spots treated the three opposition parties as a single entity and featured slogans such as "Don't let them bury your dreams" and "Don't let them send your tax cuts up in smoke." Another spot featured a set of traffic lights flashing indeterminately, representing the left–wing coalition's inability to make decisions. The tactic was repeated in spots late in National's 1999 campaign with balloons representing the three potential coalition partners, this time including the Green Party. Inter–party cooperation as a campaign tactic thus goes beyond the issues of vote–splitting and trigger electorates. It becomes a necessity for building a public perception that parties can work effectively and compatibly together once the campaigns are over.

During the 1999 campaigns it was also clear that lessons of cooperation had been learned through the mistakes of the first MMP election. Inter–party cooperation between potential coalition partners was much more common than in 1996. This time the Alliance's overall strategy was to ensure that they were a part of an Alliance/Labour government (McCarten, 2000) and their advertisements featured the slogan "heart of a new government." These two parties reached a general agreement well prior to the election and cooperated throughout most of the campaign period. Even in the televised debates, the two leaders, Clark and Anderton, worked as a team with the result that subsequent press stories reported the rapport that was evident between the two.

The message of co–operation between Labour and the Alliance during the 1999 campaign was limited, however, by the need for each party to maximise its party vote. The Alliance's poll rating rose considerably after the televised debates but that rise was at the expense of Labour (McCarten, 2000). Labour had campaigned primarily for a victory for the center–left but they had to change their strategy because of a combination of factors: very late in the campaign, there was evidence of continued voter confusion over the relevance of the party vote, exacerbated by the Alliance's campaign messages that urged support for Labour in the electorates and corresponding support for the Alliance with the party vote. Labour eventually responded with Clark's telling voters: "If you support Labour please vote for us. Don't try to find us a coalition partner with the party vote," as reported in *The Dominion*, 26 November 1999.

Very shortly before the election, Labour billboards in key electorates that depicted the local candidate had the following message pasted over them: "Only a Party Vote for Labour can change the Govt."

The comfortable relationship that had been apparent between Labour and the Alliance in 1999 was also strained by Labour's somewhat reluctant support of the Green Party in a trigger electorate. The Greens could not be assured of passing the 5–percent threshold and so needed to win an electorate seat. When Labour, very late in the campaign, communicated through the media their tacit endorsement of the Green candidate in that electorate, however, it created a problem as the Alliance did not want to have to accommodate the Greens within a Lab–our/Alliance coalition (Laugesen, 1999). From Labour's perspective, the Greens may have been needed to provide sufficient numbers for a center–left coalition. Ultimately, it did not affect the formation of government as the Greens gave support on issues of supply and confidence from outside of a coalition agreement.

Both National and the Alliance strategically withdrew or withheld candidates in 1999 to avoid splitting the right or left vote, respectively. Act also put aside its candidates in two electorates in favor of its natural coalition partner, National. In spite of that, however, Act also chose tactically to campaign aggressively against National. Act wanted to be seen as a safeguard against National's going into coalition with New Zealand First again. Act also wanted to build up its own party vote, which it could only do at National's expense. Act's justification for attacking National was given by the party's campaign director who said that Act and National did not have an "anti–democratic, anti–hostility pact like Labour and the Alliance" (Venter, 1999). The tactic extended to attacking National in the first televised debate.

The 2002 election saw yet another strategy employed by Labour in regard to campaigning against potential coalition partners. Earlier in the year Labour's existing partner, the Alliance, had split into two factions leaving each with little chance of significant representation in Parliament after the election. The Greens, the only other party of the left with sufficient support to cross the 5–percent threshold had already publicly delivered an ultimatum that it would withdraw all support, including crucial votes of confidence and monetary supply, if a Labour government were to lift the ban on field trials of genetically modified organisms once the existing moratorium expired in late 2003. Labour, relying on its own voter support rated by polls as being over 50 percent, took the high–risk strategy of campaigning for a mandate to form a majority government, with potentially only one other MP in coalition—the former leader of the Alliance, Jim Anderton, who now headed the very newly formed Progressive Coalition party. The overall reaction of voters to this strategy is discussed in Chapter Two. In terms of tactics, however, it meant that Labour had to revert to attacking a potential coalition partner. In fact, to varying degrees, Labour attacked all three of its other potential partners: the Greens, New Zealand First, and the now— reduced Alliance. As already evidenced by previous campaigns, the tactic was risky and did not work as it left voters in doubt that Labour and the Greens could negotiate their way through differences in order to form together a stable coalition government. New Zealand First had already been firmly dismissed by Labour as a partner and the Alliance was unlikely to cross the 5–percent threshold. The very late and unexpected rise in support (see Chapter Two) for an alternative coalition partner, United Future, gave voters another option for attempting to achieve a stable government and meant that Labour did not have to withdraw its attacks. It is certainly arguable that Labour's attacks, together with a refusal by the Greens to compromise, made the rise of United Future's leader, Peter Dunne, stronger than it would have otherwise been because voters wanted a coalition government as well as stability; this message of "common sense" had strong appeal.

Intra–party tensions: the electorate vs. the party vote

As alluded to above, a further issue that campaign managers had failed to come to terms with by the time of the first MMP election was that of intra–party tensions between list and electoral candidates, particularly in the two major parties. Under first–past–the–post, because the objective was to win as many electorate seats as possible, extra campaign resources were put into marginal electorates where the election result was likely to be close. Those resources generally took the form of visits by party leaders to provide visible party support and endorsement through media photo opportunities for the local candidate, and funding. Under MMP, however, campaign resources are generally put into maximizing the party vote nationwide rather than into supporting electorate candidates. The exceptions to this practice occur when, in the case of a minor party, one or two trigger electorate seats are key to the party's overall success, or if a major party decides on a tactic of trying to prevent a pivotal electorate win by a minor party candidate who could allow his or her party to enter an opposing coalition.

The overall shift in resources toward winning the party vote in 1996 caused resentment amongs electoral candidates who felt betrayed and unsupported by their party. For National Party candidates, this resentment was increased when the key party campaign message shifted from an early focus on "two ticks National," denoting a request for both votes, to "one tick National," asking only for the party vote. In order to reassure the constituency candidates, particularly those in Auckland electorates where polls revealed that Act was taking some of the party vote from National, the National Party published two advertisements in regional newspapers. The first carried a modified National Party slogan: "First Tick National; But Tick It Twice." The second, published the day before the election, stated "A vote for any other party is a vote against National." The National Party published the advertisements to reassure constituency candidates, as well as those party members, who believed that the National campaign was not being proactive enough to try and stop voters from giving their party vote to Act, particularly in Wellington Central (personal communication, 30 October 1966).

The Alliance, although a minor party, stood candidates in every electorate. This practice, and the party's reluctance to upset the candidates, was, to a large degree, the cause of the Alliance's campaign focus on the electorate rather than the party vote. Although all of its electorate candidates were also on the party list, very few could expect to enter Parliament by that route.

When the change to proportional representation was being considered, party lists were promoted as offering the opportunity to bring a wider range of representation of women and minority groups as well as required specialist expertise into Parliament without having to rely on electorate support. This was strongly reflected in Labour's single, but often repeated, television commercial of the 1996 campaign which depicted a wide range of men, women, and different ethnic representatives quietly taking their places as directors in a "board room." However, by 1999 there was a general tendency for existing MPs to also be placed on their party list. This approach was in direct response to the conflict between list and electorate candidates during the 1996 election campaign. Labour did, however, place two additional candidates high on its list to fill gaps in expertise in law and Maori affairs.

For the 2002 election, all of Labour's existing MPs were on the party list whereas National's list introduced five newcomers. The reasons for this were strategic. Labour was ranked highly in the opinion polls and did not need to change. National, on the other hand, was registering very low ratings and was attempting to revive its image. Several long–serving National MPs, reported to have been persuaded to step down from politics by the party president, Michelle Boag, had been replaced by new candidates most of whom already had high personal profiles. Her actions certainly did generate a lot of criticism from within party ranks, echoing the problems of 1996.

The issues regarding party lists differ between minor and major parties. As stated, the Alliance created difficulties for itself in 1996 by standing candidates in each electorate and focusing on them in what was essentially a first–past–the–post campaign. In 1999 most of the viable minor parties adopted a tactic of standing as many electorate candidates as possible, but this time in order to boost their party vote. Although media coverage of local electorate candidates was minimal, it was generally understood that where there was an identifiable candidate, policies were more likely to be supported. Furthermore, the Greens picked up on a tactic, which had been successfully adopted by Act in 1996, of declaring high rates of popularity as a means of creating a perception that their candidate could win a key electorate seat. The implication of such a perception was that voters would know that their party vote would count. If the electorate candidate was not perceived to be viable, the party votes would be seen as wasted. The same tactic was used again in 2002 by the new leader of the Alliance, Laila Harre, when she announced that a private poll had placed her in the lead in Waitakere, a trigger electorate for the Alliance. It was over that poll that Labour leader, Helen Clark, attacked the Alliance, accusing them of having fabricated the results.

Party differentiation and identity: a marketing problem

Under any electoral system political parties need to differentiate themselves from their opponents during, and even between, election campaigns and to communicate, most often via the media, their separate stances to voters. If they do not do so voters will not be able to choose between parties. Indeed, as discussed in the Introduction to Part One, the apparent lack of a choice between parties or candidates can be regarded as anti–democratic, and can be the reason for low voter turnout at elections (Mouffe, 1993). Catch–all political parties, often a feature of campaign modernization, that seek to capture the "middle ground" of public opinion on a range of issues, will often find themselves having to compete with at least one other party that is adopting the same or a very similar stance on the same issues. As described in the Introduction to Part Two, when issues are thus neutralized, differentiation of candidates and parties tends to be made by personality. Because proportional representation extends the viable competition during election campaigns to a range of minor parties, voters are able to cast a vote for a party that takes a strongly partisan stance on a range of issues, or one that identifies itself on the basis of a single issue, and know that their vote can be influential. Furthermore, the successful major party knows that it is likely to have to enter into a post–election coalition with a minor party and that the price of coalition will be a negotiated response to the minor party's key principles. For these reasons, the tendency toward catch–all parties is reduced under systems of proportional representation.

It is not just the electoral system that affects the degree to which political parties can cluster in the ideological center. The social and historical context of individual countries clearly plays a key role. When MMP was introduced New Zealand voters were deeply dissatisfied with the ideological directions that had been taken by National and Labour over the past decade. Indeed, it is generally accepted that their dissatisfaction was the reason that voters elected to change their electoral system (see Chapter Two). Under such circumstances, political parties are forced to take an ideologically and issues–based stance rather than cluster in the political center. This has been a particular feature of New Zealand's election campaigns over the past two decades. Any description or analysis of New Zealand's parliamentary election campaign strategies and messages, therefore, has to be framed by reference to parties' strategic positioning on ideological grounds.

The New Zealand Labour Party faced more problems in asserting its identity, based on ideological grounds, than most parties. While, as mentioned above, Labour had in many respects adopted the campaign blueprint used by Clinton in the United States and Blair's New Labour Party in Britain, it was limited in its ability to do so by the advent of MMP and because of the political history of New Zealand. Two of the key characteristics of Clinton's political strategy that were adopted for the Blair/New Labour election campaign of 1997 were "the occupation of the center ground of politics, requiring the abandonment of any historical baggage that makes the party beholden to forces associated with political extremes" and "the jettisoning of firmly held policy positions which may attract negative comment in favor of all–encompassing general statements which can be accepted by audiences with widely varying, and even conflicting, demands and which will change with public opinion" (Michie, 1998, p. 283). Blair's unwanted "baggage" was the old Labour's traditional association with the trade union movement, an association that was clearly broken by New Labour.

The New Zealand Labour Party could not follow Blair's example. In New Zealand, the historical "baggage" was primarily those former MPs of the 1984 Labour Government who were key to the neo–liberal economic reforms and who had now formed Act. Also, the New Zealand Labour Party had to deal with the other end of the political spectrum, represented by the Alliance, because it was the Alliance who was presumed to be their future coalition partner. As in Britain, neo–liberal ideology had become entrenched in New Zealand business circles and was endorsed by a relatively strong economy, yet, unlike Britain, the public clearly did not condone a continuation of privatization. Following an increasingly central path has been difficult for Labour as public opinion has kept it too left of center. Labour has had to communicate support for labor reform while distancing itself from trade unionism of the past as well as send positive messages to the business sector. In doing so, Labour has arguably based its identity upon "Third Way" principles to a greater degree than either of its allies in the United States and Britain.

While the external social and political environment has an impact on the ways in which a political party can position itself, the party's internal environment also plays an important part. Party members must be united in the dissemination of campaign messages and must exhibit internal party stability. Not only is any disunity, because of its newsworthiness, likely to be picked up by the media and communicated to voters, its coverage is likely to be given preference over any planned campaign messages. In 1996 Labour suffered from a second source of tension and message diversion among its candidates, which was much more publicly acknowledged than any generated by resource distribution and party lists. In spite of efforts to position Clark as a "prime minister in waiting," its own social history conspired against it in terms of tension over leadership. Two previous Labour prime ministers remained as MPs: one, David Lange was due for retirement; the other, Mike Moore, contested the 1996 election with the Labour

Party, although his continued allegiance to Labour was in doubt. Moore, a popular and somewhat charismatic leader, had been deposed by Clark in a bitter coup shortly after the 1993 general election. Moore was subsequently outspoken in his criticism of Labour and as late as March 1996 he considered forming his own party, reportedly with two National MPs. Speculation as to his intentions was widely aired by the press, diverting Labour's key messages and causing further damage to the Party. Moore remained with Labour but was supported by senior Labour MPs who in June 1996 asked Clark to step down in favor of Moore. The attempted coup apparently brought ideological differences within the party to the surface. Certainly, the press focused on the dissent, making cohesive communication impossible. Clark was reported in *The Dominion* on 1 June, 1996 to have described the coup attempt as the "last gasp of Rogernomics" and accused Act's leader, Richard Prebble, of working with the plotters. The accusations served to remind the voting public of Labour's remaining right–wing faction. The proponents of the attempted coup were adamant, however, that their motivation was one of wanting a popular and telegenic leader for the campaign. Patricia Herbert reported in *The New Zealand Herald* on 15 June, 1996 that:

> The Rogernomics scenario was also misleading as it implied the dispute was philosophical whereas it was only about Helen Clark—whether she should be replaced or allowed to lead Labour into the October 12 elections. The party's polling shows that she is a liability as voters are tending to use their list vote as a presidential vote or as a leader's vote.

The argument was, thus, that in the case of party leaders, personality was more important than policy in attracting the party vote. Ironically, Labour's rise in popularity later in the campaign was attributed to Clark's personal performance in the two leaders' debates broadcast on national television (Roper, 1999).

The coup itself undermined the party's own campaign messages. Ruth Laugesen of *The Dominion* reported on 1 June, 1996: "Labour plans to portray itself in the election as the only credible alternative to National, a claim that will be undermined by disunity" and on 4 June: "Labour's recurrent leadership tremors have become part of the public face of the party, reinforcing impressions of a party plagued with self–doubt."

The other influential former Labour leader, David Lange, also undermined the consistency and unity of party messages. Throughout the year he wrote a fortnightly newspaper column in which he chose to pursue a personal rather than party agenda with a commentary of his own experiences and observations (e.g. , Lange, 1996). Although he campaigned for Labour beyond his retirement, he was reported as publicly saying that after the election it was likely that the right–wing faction of the Labour MPs could defect to the National Party and that "there was too much 'baggage, ill–will, history and madness' for a formal coalition on the left" (Clifton, 1996, p. 1). Thus, Lange, too, reinforced perceptions of Labour's disunity. He, like Moore, fueled perceptions that party divisions were derived from differing views of the stance Labour should adopt in the political field.

A lack of internal party stability causes problems regardless of the electoral system but it is, however, arguable that its effects are more strongly felt under proportional representation. The reasoning here is that voters have more alternatives to choose from compounded by a desire to see the formation of a stable coalition government. This would apply, in particular, to a minor party, as evidenced by the Alliance in 2002 when it failed to win any parliamentary seats after its highly publicized division earlier in the year.

Although proportional representation allows minor parties, more so than larger parties, to clearly differentiate themselves on a narrow range of issues, because of the likelihood of governing coalitions there is a danger in communicating too strong a stance on particular issues and leaving little or no room for policy negotiation. This was the situation that faced the New Zealand Green Party in 2002 who, as mentioned above, had taken an early and very public non–negotiable stance of refusing to allow genetically modified organisms outside of laboratories, thus excluding field trials.

Although the Greens did have policies on a range of issues, public and media interest on the genetic modification stance effectively reduced their campaign to a single issue. Their key campaign message was "only a vote for the Green Party can keep GE in the lab." As they were, at the outset of the election campaign period, the most likely coalition partner for Labour, they ran the risk of compromising Labour's stance or forcing Labour to attempt to form a minority Government. They also ran the risk that voters would withhold their votes from the Greens in favor of Labour, in order to allow Labour to form a more stable, majority government on its own. Mid–campaign polls certainly indicated that National voters were prepared to give their party votes to Labour to help avoid having to form a coalition with the Greens. On the other hand, if the Greens had compromised their core identity by giving in on the genetic modification issue, they would have lost their key differentiation for the election. They had to decide whether it was worth campaigning to be a part of government or whether they would maintain a purist stance outside of government.

The non–negotiable position taken by the Greens in 2002 echoed that of the Alliance in 1996 when their refusal to enter post–election coalition negotiations caused a problem for the party, as stated above. In terms of differentiation, the danger of pre–election coalitions was that one party's identity could too readily be merged with that of its coalition partner, while a clear advantage of withholding coalition agreements until after the election was that it was easier for a party to differentiate itself from others if it campaigned alone. The purity of the Alliance stance, once committed to, also meant that the Alliance could not campaign with the usual minority party slogans of post–election support for another party and insurance against that party's deviating from its election promises. Act's 1996 advertising, for example, promoted the party as "the honest broker in the new Parliament," while in 1999 New Zealand First's slogan was "keeping them honest." The Alliance's failure to communicate a position of a viable coalition partner for Labour, coupled with their negative campaigning against Labour, is widely believed to have lost them considerable support. Voters considered their votes wasted on a party that had already opted out of being a part of a coalition government.

By the 1999 election Alliance and Labour had already been publicly cooperating with each other for about 18 months in an effort to communicate to the voting public their ability to form a stable government together. Even their policies were aligned, most notably over the issue of taxation. In 1996 the Alliance campaigned for progressive taxation, meaning tax increases for the wealthy and reductions for the poor. For "middle New Zealand" this was perceived as a threat rather than a benefit. In 1999 the Alliance had modified its taxation policy by raising the threshold over which taxation would rise. The modified policy was not only more palatable to voters but was now consistent with Labour policy. The united message of these parties of the left and center–left was appreciated by voters, as was their unity as a coalition government. However, a comment published by the Alliance campaign manager in reflection of their 1999 campaign was prophetic. He stated "If we cannot differentiate ourselves from our coalition partner over the next three years, then we will be in grave trouble at the next election" (McCarten, 2000, p. 40). The accuracy of his statement was seen in the split of the Alliance before the 2002 election. The same pre–election concern about a potential inability to differentiate that led to a loss of voter support in 1996 led to an even greater loss of support in 2002 when the concern was perceived to have become a reality. The other faction of the Alliance, later to become the Progressive Coalition (under Jim Anderton), had argued that an election campaign based on a continuing position as a stable coalition partner for Labour was viable.

Differentiation and identity positioning of political parties through election campaign messages is more complex under proportional representation than under majoritarian electoral systems. While modern technology and global expertise can help identify and target key voter groups, many factors relating to an individual party's own identity as well as those of its potential coalition partners must be factored in. Specific campaign messages that are disseminated through advertisements, press releases, and speeches are tailored to specific parties for each election. However, the common strategies that drive these messages are discernible. The emerging pattern is that the messages must convey stability of the party, unity of coalition, and clear differentiation from other parties. In New Zealand it is still the case that campaign messages must be predominantly issues–based and reflect each party's ideological stance. Leadership has remained a key factor both as a stabilizing force within each party and as a focus for media, as described below.

Campaigning and the media

As elsewhere in the world, New Zealand politicians depend upon media coverage to disseminate their campaign messages as widely and as favorably as possible and, conversely, it is through the media that voters learn most about their politicians and their campaigns. The type of information disseminated, however, varies according to whether the messages are "controlled" or "uncontrolled." The use of mass media, in the form of paid advertisements and Party Political Broadcasts using allocated television broadcasting time, allow control over the form and content of message in line with party strategy. It does not, however, lend the same legitimacy to the messages as the uncontrolled forms such as news, documentaries, and debates. News coverage is thus so important that politicians, especially the party leaders, schedule their daily campaign activities to provide photo opportunities for accompanying journalists as well as to ensure availability for evening television news broadcasts. Not only does this arrangement suit party leaders in terms of not having to deliver their messages in person around the county, it also suits the media preference for personalized stories that focus on an elite individual. In this regard, the leader focus takes on many characteristics of a presidentialized or personalized campaign, aimed primarily at the party vote. Personalization thus occurs in New Zealand for two key reasons: the preference of the media to frame their stories around one "elite" figure, and to provide a focus for the campaign drive for the party vote. Personalization can also be said to occur through the electorate campaigns where the local candidate is highlighted, but these campaigns receive little national media coverage. In many cases where a local candidate is not well known, advertisements will picture the local candidate alongside the Party leader as a means of endorsement.

Party Political Broadcasts, which deliver controlled messages targeted primarily toward the party vote, predominantly feature the party leader. The ways in which these broadcasts are developed depend upon both time allocation and resources for production. For the major parties whose allocation of time is greatest (around 30 minutes), it can be a problem to fill the time and maintain public interest. National and Labour, who have both the largest time allocation and the greatest resources, produce increasingly sophisticated broadcasts, featuring the party leaders but in a variety of contexts and in relation to a range of issues. The remainders of these longer broadcasts tend to feature the spokespeople for the major portfolios such as health and education as well as a range of candidates from a demographic perspective in order to appeal to as wide a range of potential voters as possible. For the smaller, less well–funded parties with a much shorter allocation of time, the party leaders will often feature throughout the broadcast.

While for some parties the political broadcasts are considered unnecessarily long, the other form of television advertising, the campaign spot, is necessarily short because of funding limitations. The campaigns feature a mixture of negative and positive spots although the positive ones have been more common over the past three campaigns. In 1996, Labour produced only the one spot which was positive and in 1999 only one negative spot among a range of positive ones. The negative spots tend to be aired late in the campaigns and this was certainly the case for National in both 1996 and 1999. In each of these campaigns, National's negative spots depicted an unstable coalition of the three left of center parties, as described above, while the positive ones focused either on the party leader as a stable and capable leader, or on one of National's potential ministers.

In the case of uncontrolled media coverage, also as elsewhere, the relationship between the New Zealand media and politicians is not an easy one as each pursues different agenda. While politicians vie for media coverage of their campaigns and policies, journalists want to be seen to retain their independence and objectivity, although the degree to which election campaign reporting can be said to actually be objective is questionable, in spite of the fact that New Zealand does not have an overtly partisan press as exists in Britain. The publicly owned television Channel One has an obligation to cover the election and the other, privately owned Channel Three imposes that same obligation upon itself so that both national channels provide a range of programs designed to inform and engage voters with election issues. It is relevant that each of these channels, despite their very different types of ownership, is run on a competitive, commercial basis.

The second dominant feature of media coverage of New Zealand election campaigns is that stories are frequently couched in terms of winners and losers, based upon the results of opinion polls. Again, this in line with international trends is commonly referred to as "horserace journalism." One form of such journalism that stands out is the televised debate where politicians, usually party leaders, are pitted against each other and a winner is declared at the end.

Televised debates between party leaders during political election campaigns are well–established institutions internationally. In New Zealand in 1996, however, Channel One introduced what became widely known as "the worm." The worm was, in reality, a graph of the averaged opinions of a group of uncommitted voters who, as they watched the debates, registered their reactions with a hand held meter. The graph was shown on the television screen superimposed over replayed "highlights" of the debate and was also used to rank the leaders from winner to loser. With some differences in format the technique was used again for the televised debates of the 2002 campaigns. In each case, the worm provided both an entertainment format for the debates and what was treated as a scientific and objective measure of performance. Each use of the worm was followed by a stream of press stories that largely had the effect of reducing election campaign coverage to leaders' respective performances as judged by the worm. The result of the prolonged press coverage of the debates was significant. In 1996, it was credited with a rise in popularity for Labour's Helen Clark and a downturn for National (see Roper, 1999).

In 2002 the use of the device was again credited with instigating a turnaround, much more spectacular than in 1996, of the prospects of a political party shortly before the election. The United Future Party, led by Peter Dunne, had not been successful at getting media coverage prior to the debate. During the debate, the undecided voters whose responses were being translated into "the worm" responded favorably to Dunne's middle–of–the–road stance and apparently "commonsense" arguments. He was declared the winner of the debate, a dubious call in itself as New Zealand First's leader, Winston Peters, had appeared to be rated on a par with Dunne. From then until the election the press gave much more exposure to Dunne, using headlines such as "Worm

Debate Makes Dunne Powerbroker" (Mold and Armstrong, 2002). Dunne's rating in the opinion polls rose sharply in the following few days, with at least one poll taking him from 1.1 percent to 6.6 percent within five days.

What the media failed to do, arguably because of their preference for predicting winners and coalitions, was to inform voters about the policies and nature of United Future. This is a party that first campaigned in 1996, with very limited success, as the United Party under Dunne and had undergone major changes of its party list candidates in subsequent elections. By 2002 the party had joined with Future New Zealand, a Christian party. Seven United Future list candidates entered Parliament with Dunne, most of them from Future New Zealand. Commentary about these candidates, however, emerged only after the election, when they were labeled as right–wing, although they had been voted in as a viable centrist coalition partner for Labour. It is doubtful that many voters were even aware of the religious views and strongly moralistic stances of several of the elected candidates.

New Zealand's political parties, as well as its voters, are adapting to the new electoral system, although it is apparent that mistakes are still being made. Many of the campaign strategies and tactics echo those developed elsewhere in the world and are developed in response to the availability of new technologies, expertise, and the demands of media. Yet, while principles are emerging that are generally relevant, there is no campaign blueprint that can be universally applied. What is also apparent is that the media plays a dominant role in determining which aspects of a party's campaign will be most widely publicized, which will be ignored, and how the stories will be told.

Chapter Six

Italy: Playing the Majoritarian and Looking at the Proportional

As in several other liberal democracies, electoral campaigning patterns and practices in Italy have changed significantly over the past 20 years. Many factors of change have been pointed out by comparative research (Swanson and Mancini, 1996): structural and systemic as well as cultural and contingent variables worked in many political contexts to prompt political subjects (e.g., parties, leaders, politicians, candidates) to update their ways of gathering political consensus. Among these factors the mediatization of politics and political communication stands out as one of the major thrusts toward the modernization of campaigning (Mazzoleni and Schulz, 1999).

In the Italian case, as will be described below, perhaps the foremost independent variable of the change is to be found in the momentous switch from the pure proportional electoral system to the mixed PL–PR system of representation (see Chapter Three). The predominantly majoritarian rule, introduced in 1993 and applied for the first time in the general election of 1994, represented a revolution for the country's political system and consequently forced political actors to resort to new but, not entirely unprecedented (see Mazzoleni, 1991) forms and formats of campaign strategies. However, the changes in the electoral rules themselves were, to a certain extent, provoked—or encouraged— by the mounting commercialization of Italian society and of political communication. Signs of what have been labeled the "berlusconization" of Italian politics, after the 1994 electoral victory of the media mogul Silvio Berlusconi, could indeed be spotted in the changing media climate of the country years before his first electoral success. Berlusconi contributed noticeably to the commercialization of the Italian way of life through his three major television channels and by placing television at the center of the political arena. His spectacular entrance into that arena in 1994, following the crumbling of the old political system under the hammers of judicial actions for corruption (the so–called *Tangentopoli*), was later to be regarded as a natural finale to his amazing road show in the country's media industry and economy.

Most political parties and politicians, faced with the introduction of a significant majoritarian quota in the electoral system, easily—and at times enthusiastically—converted to new campaign communication patterns, either because it meant a refurbishing of their worn–out image or because they could not help renovating their campaign machines, lest they be left behind in the electoral race. So, in a way, one may say that in Italy the introduction of the plurality system triggered the modernization of campaigning practices. However, this does not necessarily mean that all the political actors easily and eagerly embraced the new rules of the electoral game. On the contrary, resistance to it was especially common to the parties that had survived the collapse of the political system of the early 1990s or to their direct descendants. Such opposition was, of course, rather odd, as these parties had contributed in Parliament to pass the reform in 1993, and had previously endorsed the outcomes of the popular referendum in favor of the majoritarian. As observed in Chapter Three, public opinion in the first half of the decade had manifested a clear turn toward political stability and a strong demand for simplification of the political spectrum. The fragmentation of the political forces in Parliament was blamed as the culprit for the structural instability of Italian governments (about 50 cabinets in just as many years).

While adhering without enthusiasm to the changed mood of the national electorate, a number of parties (especially the smallest ones from the ex–DC, Christian Democratic center, and from the left) withstood the drift to the majoritarian—which signified for them the risk of disappearing—and began to lobby for a return to full proportional rule. In the meantime, they attempted to get the most advantage from the new system by means of astute negotiations before joining a parent coalition (for the candidatures in the single–member districts) and especially by trying to besiege the 25 percent proportional quota.

Of course, things changed along with the succession of legislatures. Even early pro–majoritarian parties like Berlusconi's *Forza Italia* and Bossi's Northern League turned pro–proportional in the debate after their defeat in 1996, but reconverted to the majoritarian system following their latest victory in the 2001 general elections.

The somersaults in the attitudes of new and old parties are not merely a function of the strength of their contingent political interests; rather, they are, correlated to the degree of success of the (slow) consolidation of bi–polarism (i.e., the Italian version of the two–party system, often depicted by opinion leaders as the panacea to the infirmity of the country's political system). In fact, looking at the three elections held with the mixed plurality–proportional rule (PL–PR), we can see that in 1994 "the degree of fragmentation of the party system remained very high; the behavior of the parties and eventually of the electorate was still tied to a proportional logic" (Bartolini and D'Alimonte, 2002, p. 9). In 1996 the majority in Parliament of the victorious center–left was too thin and the coalition was unstable because of the tensions between the parties that compounded it. Finally, in 2001, the elections "have yielded a clear–cut majority in both Chambers and have also 'punished' . . . the 'third–force' ambitions of those who resist the bi–polar transformation of the Italian party system" (p. 10).

The uncertainties in the attitudes of Italy's political parties regarding the new mixed majoritarian–proportional system are mirrored also in the practicalities of running election campaigns. This explains the title of this chapter and is described and discussed in the sections that follow.

When a hyper–proportional rule yielded mostly figurative campaigns

In the so–called First Republic, that is, in the almost five decades of Italy's political life conditioned by the pure proportional vote, election campaigns pursued the goal of asserting and confirming the existing identity of the political factions engaged in the contest rather than of conquering new consensus.

From the 1950s on, the electoral maps revealed a fairly rigid voting dynamic that was labeled by political scientists: "mobility without movement" (Parisi, 1980). The variations in vote outcomes had little significance overall; that is, they were never able to overturn the existing power balances. Two mass parties, the DC and the Communist Party (PCI), dominated the scene and their enduring contraposition affected the political strategies of the other parties, especially the Socialist Party (PSI) which was condemned to be allied with the DC, as without them the latter would not have an absolute majority in Parliament.

The First Republic was, in its own way, a stable system. That is, it was characterized by government coalitions without any real alternation. The DC was always the leading governing party, the PSI was almost always its major partner, and the PCI was always excluded from government. The former leading politician Aldo Moro called this situation "frozen democracy."

The Cold War climate of those decades explains most of this peculiar pattern of Italian politics. Other peculiarities are to be found in the fierce ideological conflict between moderate and leftist forces, in the stable electoral balances of the major political subjects (the DC's electoral support averaged 30 percent, the PSI's 10 percent, and the PCI's 25 percent), and in the fairly strong political participation; voting turnout was around 90 percent in all election contests of the period.

How such stable dynamics could generate so much turbulence in the governing quarters, to the point of counting dozens of cabinets in almost 50 years, is a question that has to do with the shortcomings of the existing proportional electoral system. Because of the lack of any threshold, the tiniest political formations could easily gain crucial parliamentary seats, thus yielding a fragmented Parliament that made it difficult for the relative–majority party (i.e., DC) to form strong, tight government coalitions. It goes without saying that these small parties tried to gain the most out of their pivotal power, often provoking government crises.

Research has identified three distinctive voting patterns of the First Republic (Parisi and Pasquino, 1977): the subcultural vote, the exchange vote, and the opinion vote.

The first pattern is probably the most typical of the period, as it relates to a voting behavior rooted in the strong ideological and cultural cleavages of Italian society of those years. Catholics were more likely to vote for the DC party, the voters living in the traditionally red (communist) regions would vote for the PCI, the non–Christian, non–communist voters would support the PSI, and so on. This kind of partisanship explained most of the lack of electoral volatility of the First Republic.

The second pattern, the exchange vote, or the clientele–based voting behavior, was quite diffused, especially in southern Italy, where the governing parties were keener to exchange favors for votes. This pattern was also typical of the period and was a good predictor of voting trends. Endemic political corruption was just one step away from the exchange vote, as the subsequent phase of *Tangentopoli* revealed.

Finally, the opinion vote pattern referred to a voting behavior prompted by the personal evaluation of a political platform and of government performance—very much influenced by the flow of information in the news media.

While the first two patterns explained most of the voting trends, the third one was the weakest predictor. However, research into election results monitored a slow but steady increase of its significance until the eve of the Second Republic (see Parisi and Schadee, 1995).

Under similar conditions, the potential of major gains by any contender in the Italian political arena was indeed very scanty. Accordingly, the electoral competitions were not primarily aimed at acquiring new converts. They were more like celebrations, confirmation rituals of parties' own identities. In fact, the major as well as minor parties and the governing as well as opposition forces all endeavored to mark their ideological differences, to defend their positions and pivotal power, and to ensure continuity of the existing order. The proportional rule guaranteed all parties participation in the benefits of the so–called consociationalism/ *consociativismo*. That is, the unwritten, unspoken, but tangible convergence of interests among government majorities and opposition parties by which the latter would publicly oppose certain policies while indirectly contributing to their approval in Parliament in exchange for support and power.

Election campaigns in the 1950s

Electioneering of the pure proportional era evolved along with modernization of communication techniques. However, in the first decade after World War Two, the competing parties showed little regard for searching for fancier and more effective tools. In the heated general election of 1948, the first democratic contest of the

Republican era, there was the choice between freedom and Soviet communism. The elections of the ensuing period reflected the stabilizing of the irreconcilable divide between the ruling center–right and the strong socialist–communist opposition. The political parties, engaged in the campaigns of 1953 and 1958, emphasized their ideological differences. The old campaign techniques had worked marvelously in all previous campaigns, including the local contests: imaginative posters, mass rallies, and door–to–door canvassing were the main communication channels of the time. Notes Luciano Cheles:

> The poster is a quintessential Italian medium. Its widespread use as a means of mobilization may be explained in the light of the Catholic Church's centuries–old tradition of using artistic forms for persuasive ends. . . . It should, moreover, be related to the outdoor nature of much of recreational life of Italy: the ritual of the *passeggiata* (strolling) alone justifies the parties' investment in this form of communication. . . . Before the advent of television, this medium provided political movements with strong visual characterization, especially through the depiction of party emblems, thus rendering them more easily recognizable by the electorate (2001 p. 125).

Election campaigns in the 1960s

The inauguration of television in Italian election campaigns took place in 1960, when a major local election was called. For the first time the leaders of the parties confronted each other and the journalists transposing the typical rhetorical formats of the squabbles between political adversaries from the public squares to the television studios. Slowly the politicians gave up their excessively aggressive manners and adjusted to the grammar of the new medium and to the limitations and constraints devised by the government–controlled public service broadcasting company. However, television had little significant effect on the campaign style of the decade, which still largely relied on traditional techniques. In the campaigns of 1963 and 1968, political propaganda demonstrated only a lukewarm attention to more modern communication formats.

There was no sign of exploitation of the charismatic personal leadership or concession to the portrayal of the personalities of the leaders. The posters were still weapons for ideological conflicts: they depicted abstract themes such as freedom, family, peace, socialism, and reforms; this very much the same as those of the previous decade. The change could rather be seen in the less apocalyptic tone of such messages. The propaganda of the PCI of those de–Stalinization years was no longer menacing, with the dark colors disappearing. The DC presented itself as the face of a 20–year–old woman ("*La DC ha vent'anni*," was the heading of this famous poster). This Christian Democratic propaganda is the earliest example of a still awkward attempt to modernize campaign weaponry. In fact, the party resorted to an American advertising agency for its 1963 campaign. The poster, however, was a bit ahead of its time, and it boomeranged, throwing ridicule on the party. The domestic political struggle was clearly not yet ready to convert to more modern communication models.

Election campaigns in the 1970s

The elections during this decade were in 1972, 1976, and 1979. These were years of social unrest and economic setback as the country faced a period of terrorism. The political life of Italy was marked by vehement conflicts, even among allied parties. The agenda of the tumultuous public debate did not include the reform of the electoral system. On the government front, the allied parties gave birth to 13 cabinets in 10 years, all headed by Christian Democratic prime ministers.

The 1972 general election campaign was distinguished by its contrast with the climate of social unrest in the country. Paradoxically it could be considered an "American–like" example of a campaign. It was extremely noisy, extravagant, and expensive. Public opinion was scandalized by such a demonstration of political insensitivity. Parliament passed a bill (No. 130) in 1975 to simplify campaigning, fixing the length to 30 days and prohibiting a series of invasive audiovisual techniques. The return to more sober customs was actually prompted by the oil crisis of the early 1970s that imposed a mantle of austerity on the country's lifestyle.

In the same year (1975) Parliament had approved a more important law which was bound to trigger significant changes in the coming years in the general political balances. Bill No. 103, labeled the "Reform of RAI," took control of the public broadcasting company away from government and entrusted it to Parliament. A special parliamentary board, in which all major and minor parties were to be proportionally represented, would have the task, among others, of regulating access to public television and radio channels and to oversee the use of these public channels in campaigns. The same law unintentionally sparked the rush of private enterprises to commercial broadcasting by allowing the establishment of local cable television stations. These enterprises succeeded in getting a ruling of the Constitutional Court (No. 202) in 1976 that liberalized broadcasting—even if only on the local level.

The immediate effect of such deliberation by the Court was the experimental use of electoral television commercials in the 1976 campaigns, aired by a small number of local stations. Very few voters had the chance to watch these unprecedented political ads, but it was the first time in the history of Italian campaigning and the beginning of revolution in overhauling traditional campaign communication formats.

It is worth noting that in all campaigns from 1948–1989 that the proportional system allowed multi–preference voting that favored intense competition, even among candidates of the same party list, and "led them to outdo one another with gimmicks in an attempt to attract the attention of the public and secure their preferences. Hence the elaborate ways in which many chose to have themselves represented in posters and other literature" (Cheles, 2001, p. 158), and from then on, also in television commercials.

Election campaigns in the 1980s

The parliamentary elections of the 1980s were held in 1983, 1987, and 1989. None of those elections was called at the completion of the statutory 5–year term. The permanently conflicting relations among the allied parties neither facilitated the natural expiration of the legislatures, nor the formation of stable cabinets. However, for the first time in post–war politics, a non–DC premier was appointed. Bettino Craxi, the strongman of the PSI, succeeded in leading the coalition in spite of the fact that his party had only 13 percent (vis–à–vis the DC's 25 percent) of the vote. His cabinet achieved the record for duration (by traditional Italian standards): more than three years, from 1983–1987.

The election campaign of 1983 was a milestone in the modernization of Italian political and electoral communication. By the mid–1980s, commercial television was established as a permanent feature in the Italian media system (see Pezzini, 2001). The rhetorical devices of television commercial advertising, swiftly adopted by candidates, took the place of traditional, emotionally based party propaganda forms. Access to commercial stations, unlike public service broadcasting channels, was unrestricted and unregulated. Parties and politicians exploited these new communication resources extensively. The volume of campaign advertising, and electoral broadcasts in general, increased to the point that election contests were associated with television–centered campaigning.

It is during those years that campaign practices underwent a remarkable change: researchers began to notice the first signs of a process of *Americanization*, or spectacularization of politics and campaign communication (for examples see Statera, 1986; Mazzoleni, 1987). The most tangible changes were in the decline of rallies in public squares which were supplanted by appearances on television broadcasts, the adoption of marketing techniques such as targeted mailings, and the use of communication consultants. The image of both parties and candidates became paramount in campaign communications at the expense of the traditional predilection for ideological and policy issues. All this represented a change in the traditional temperament of the Italian political communication. The marketing mentality prompted a more proselytist outlook in campaign strategies. That is, parties slowly moved from the preservation–directed attitude of the previous decades to one more conquest–directed; thus anticipating some trends that would be more evident later in the 1990s when the mixed PL–PR electoral system was inaugurated.

It should be observed that the crisis of the old political establishment begins in the 1980s and during this time the pressure to introduce institutional reforms intensified, although with minimal results, because of the resistance of a significant part of the country's political class. In a word, it was a decade of groundwork for major changes that was made possible only thanks to the collapse of the old party system in the early 1990s.

When a mixed electoral system prompts
more competitive campaigns

The evidence described in the previous section illustrates that modernization of election campaigns is not necessarily exclusive to just one form of electoral rule. Some significant changes registered in Italy's electioneering go back to the pure proportional years (1948–1992), which simply mean that both proportional and majoritarian varieties can prompt contenders to search for fresh and sharp methods with which to present their platform. The section that follows discusses the continuation of the modernization process under the mixed PL–PR system. This process appears to be a function of technological developments in the media and communication domains, changes in the traditional patterns of political engagement and participation, and a general trend toward forms of mediatization, spectacularization, and personalization of political action.

The change in Italian campaigns accompanies the broader changes in Italian society and polity. Political parties under the hyper–proportional rule of the First Republic started to implement *real* competitive tactics only from the early 1980s even though the "frozen democracy" would not allow a genuine alternation of majority/opposition forces (see Chapter Three). Before then it had been a purely intra–coalition competition, with meager chances of conquering substantial quotas of new supporters from the adversaries' camps.

Those chances, however, increased slowly but steadily along with the secularization of the country's political sphere and the growing volatility of traditional voting behavior. The search for more antagonistic campaign tactics by political parties was a sort of instinctive adaptation to (and exploitation of) the new climate. With this background, when the revolution took place in 1993 it was also a revolution of campaign practices. Italian election campaigns had already sufficiently modernized to open the door to the spectacular inauguration of horseracing, hoop–la, and television–centered electoral competitions.

The election campaign of 1994

The 1992 elections were held under the Damocles's sword of the anti–corruption judicial actions. They are only remembered as the last elections of the so–called First Republic and for sending to

Parliament for the last time a political class that was about to be knocked out by the arrests and trials of dozens of politicians and party leaders. Most of these arrests were in the precincts of the parties that had ruled the country for the past 40–plus years.

On the wave of the national drama of what looked like the "twilight of gods" for those interminable years, the pressure of public opinion for a similar theatrical upheaval succeeded in pushing through the electoral reform of 1993 from a cowed Parliament. As observed, the mixed PL–PR system was eventually a compromise between the still many supporters of hyper–proportionalism (who were nevertheless intimidated by the nation's mood) and the fewer advocates of the majoritarian rule (who, on the contrary, felt strongly supported by this same sentiment).

The new rule was to be inaugurated in the extraordinary elections called in 1994. They were defined by the press as the first elections of the Second Republic, to suggest the innovative potential they were going to inject into the country's political life. The climate of general public opinion was indeed one of great expectation, but it was also one of widespread uncertainty, especially about which political forces would benefit most from the downfall of the old establishment. In other words, there was a serious vacuum in the political offer which equated into anxiety about the working of the new system and rumors of clandestine maneuvers to boycott the transition by the remnants of the old class.

In the midst of this rather fluid situation came the unexpected appearance of a media mogul suddenly stepping into the race with a brand new political formation manifestly intentioned to win the bid. It is probable that under the former hyper–proportional electoral rule, Berlusconi would not have had the same odds that he now enjoyed with the majoritarian features introduced by the new law. His marketing–based campaign strategies and tactics—ones that gave an exceptional spin to the modernization process of Italian election campaigns—were primarily aimed at capturing the vote in the first–past–the–post districts.

The most significant event of that campaign, however, was the launching, through a bombardment of television commercials, of *Forza Italia*, a brand new party with a center–right ideology which deliberately set out to intercept the moderate votes and the orphans of the disappeared DC and PSI parties. Unlike the traditional parties, which mainly relied on heavy party machines, *Forza Italia* had loose links with the electorate and a very light organizational structure. Researchers and analysts labeled it as a "flash party," a "light party," a "media–centered party," a "personal party" (Calise, 2000); all were attempts to define a novelty in the country's political arena in relation to its unusual multi–faceted nature. It was in fact founded for a specific, immediate goal. Its activists had no political experience and the party employed aggressive communication and marketing tools drawing its energy from its charismatic leader, Berlusconi (see Mazzoleni, 1995).

The campaign was dominated by Berlusconi (*Forza Italia)* and the coalition Pole of Freedoms/Pole of Good Government, both by their direct communication strategies and by the heated reactions of the contending coalition (*I progressisti*). It was undoubtedly an antagonistic type of campaign, mostly fought in the media and through the media. Berlusconi could influence three commercial television channels and other print media, while the opposing field relied on the endorsement of many key broadcasters and journalists of the public service channels, as well as several daily newspapers.

The new electoral rules deeply affected the way the whole campaign was conducted by the various players. It imposed a reduction in the number of forces confronting each other on the battlefield, prompting them to aggregate in large electoral coalitions. It forced candidates to adjust their campaign activities to the unprecedented single–member districts (now of about one hundred thousand inhabitants) and made it a battle of personalities rather than of issues. The two front–runners met head–to–head in a memorable "great television debate" on the eve of Election Day, thus sanctioning from then on the irreversible personalization of Italian politics. The heated confrontation between the two major players (the third minor one, the center coalition Pact for Italy did not succeed in gaining sufficient media attention) was accompanied by extraordinary popular parti-cipation in the campaign debate and in the turnout. The simplification of political competition, strongly buttressed by the media, reached its climax in 1994 as the general election of that year ended up as a sort of referendum for or against Berlusconi. There was some concern in the post–election comments about such supposedly distorted results of the plurality rule. A further significant side–effect observed by researchers was the "leaderization" of electoral communication (see Mancini and Mazzoleni, 1995), by which unknown candidates who had used little or no propaganda, were eventually voted in by a landslide in the first–past–the–post districts, just for being on the list represented by the leader, Berlusconi.

In brief, the 1994 campaign initiated a series of political and media processes that were going to mark indelibly the post– reform election campaigns.

The election campaign of 1996

The new electoral system was supposed to guarantee more stable governments by setting in motion a bi–polarization of the political spectrum and, accordingly, by leading to a clearer majority–opposition dialectic. The Berlusconi cabinet, appointed after his sweeping victory in 1994, resigned after only eight months because the *Lega Nord*, one of the major allies of his coalition, withdrew its parliamentary support. The *Lega Nord*, fearing a loss of its still strong identity (and constituency) by going along with Berlusconi's policies and leadership, walked out, defying the spirit of the reform. It was the first manifestation of major drawbacks of a reform that appeared to fail in putting an end to the old Italian tradition of Cabinet–grinding. Parties forced to join coalitions for tactical, arithmetical reasons, even in the face of hardly reconcilable idiosyncrasies, are still likely to clash when faced with strong tensions within the coalition or in the cabinet. The political/policy differences that are tactically blurred before the elections surface later in the legislature. There is no mechanism in the new electoral law to prevent further fragmentation, and no assurance that if a cabinet falls, new elections will be called promptly.

In fact after Berlusconi's fall there was a period of political ambiguity under an interim cabinet headed by Dini, a former minister of the Berlusconi government. He eventually founded his own party, *Rinnovamento Italiano*, that would exploit the proportional quota in the next elections, which were called in April 1996.

This time the political situation was completely different from that of 1994. There was no longer a political vacuum as the parties—small and big—had consolidated their grasp on the electorate and the bi–polarization evidenced by the two competing coalitions was also starting to become a familiar feature of the domestic political scene. However, the campaign for the general election of 1996 was distinguished by several somewhat unusual and unexpected factors that eventually affected the outcome. In particular, two stand out as the most conspicuous ones: the enforcement of the *"par condicio"* (impartial media treatment) regulation; and the return to more policy–centered campaign dialectics.

The president of the Republic and parties of the left wanted a regulation for fair competition in order to prevent dominant positions in the media and to guarantee equal access and media coverage for all political contenders, independent of the breadth of their constituencies. The sorry lesson of 1994, when a political leader and media tycoon had won the elections, was clearly still a burning issue for many political actors with little or no media power.

The new limitations obliged the news media to cover all campaign actors and events fairly, and prohibited candidates and parties airing paid commercials on private radio and television channels. One interesting effect of the *par condicio* regulation was the augmented and therefore assured visibility of the minor actors in the contest, especially of the small parties and obscure candidates of the proportional tier, who would otherwise have been destined for oblivion.

The overall result of the introduction of the regulation was a sober kind of campaign communication output, one more austere and low cost than that of the previous campaign. It is worth noting, though, that politicians and leaders had devised a clever way to circumvent the *par condicio* constraints: by kicking off their actual campaign warfare months ahead of the official campaign start date. Berlusconi aired his own and his coalition's commercials in the pre–campaign months, and Prodi rode the Olive Tree bus throughout Italy, securing daily news coverage from the many journalists following his campaign trail. Therefore, the more austere tones were only confined to the 30–day campaign. The trend to spectacularization of campaign practices did not stop; neither did the mediatization register a tangible decline. On the contrary, "the media and especially television confirmed their role of primary arena of the electoral battle" (Marini and Roncarolo, 1997, p. 29). The great debate between the leaders of the two opposing coalitions took place on television and was a landmark of the entire campaign. The trend to personalization received further impetus from the media, as it had for more than a decade.

The "lower key" that characterized the general tone of the 1996 campaign was also due to two specific contingencies: the novelty factor candidacy by a celebrated outsider had vanished; and, in the opposite corner, Prodi was anything but a flamboyant communicator.

All these factors contributed to move the pivot of the campaign to more substantial matters to some extent. Content analysis of the media–carried debate reveals unequivocally the pre–eminence of policy issues, such as welfare reform, balancing the budget, unemployment and job incentives, and the like, in the campaign debates (Marini and Roncarolo, 1997, p. 83). Furthermore there was mounting political pressure from organized actors from "civil society" who wanted to make their voices heard and to join the battle for the agenda control. Dealers, industrialists, and labour unions staged a series of clamorous pseudo–events, such as *Tax Day* and *Labor Day*, which succeeded in drawing the attention of the media and in imposing their issues on the political debate. The front–runners of the coalitions and leaders and spokespeople from several parties could not help tagging on issues that were successfully raised by external players.

Overall, the 1996 campaign—which ended with a victory for the Olive Tree center–left coalition—revealed that the reform of institutional mechanics does not necessarily ensure a democratic representation of the voters' will, unless warranties for a fair competition are envisaged. It also confirmed certain important trends in the political and media domains that had originated in the proportional era and had gained propulsion after the change of the electoral rule.

The election campaign of 2001

The last general elections have been considered by scholarly research as the consolidation of the new electoral system, especially of the bi–polarized political game (Bartolini and D'Alimonte, 2002). The large majority in both the Chamber of Deputies and the Senate, conquered by Berlusconi's *House of Freedoms*, the disappearance of third–force initiatives, and the alternation of coalitions in power (1994: center–right; 1996: center–left; 2001: center–right) validate the argument of most political science analysts (see Pasquino, 2002, Il Sistema...), that the new system is starting to work well in spite of its shortcomings.

The election campaigns of the transition are definitely more competitive in style than those of the proportional years. Only two major camps are expected to face each other, even if not all the troops are utterly devoted to the common cause, thanks to room left by the proportional quota to combat their own individual battles.

Looking at the campaign that preceded the 2001 ballot, one can acknowledge a sort of settlement of practices (and tricks) that have been experimented with in recent campaigns (e.g., mayoral, regional, European): the search for a prestigious, popular, and possibly media–genic personality as front–runner of a coalition; the leader dominance over candidates in the single–member districts; the candidate's image dominance over party identities (but not coalition's); the inauguration of the actual campaigning long before its statutory inception; the attempt to subdue the news media to one's strategic exigencies; and a larger professional-ization of electioneering.

The campaign waged by the center–right coalition *House of Freedoms* was marked by the acknowledged political savvy of its leader. Berlusconi strengthened his own personal party, *Forza Italia*, against all suggestions that it would soon disappear as a flash party, and showed instead that it was a powerful electoral machine. He also managed to call the *Lega Nord*, after years of mutual detestation, back into the old alliance.

On the strategic communication front, Berlusconi tried systematically to keep the whole campaign agenda under tight control. He displayed this both within his own coalition and versus the opposition coalition of the Olive Tree. Besides relying on his own long experience, he resorted to in–house professional-ism, as he had done in 1994 when he engaged the salespeople of his advertising firms to disseminate his message. Together with his closest collaborators he put up the so–called Table for Italy, a war–room that met with him every week to ensure the launch of a highly coherent campaign. The attack on adversaries was launched with two fronts: street posters and television.

Starting six months before election day Berlusconi inundated the country with large posters portraying his (younger) close–up photo with catchy phrases such as "Less taxes for all" and "Safer cities." He also utilized assertions like "A president–worker to change Italy," "A president–entrepreneur to launch great infrastructures," "A President–friend to help those who can't make it." It was a clever way to arrive first and to set the agenda of the public pre–electoral debate. Those posters triggered a response from Rutelli, leader of the Olive Tree, who lagged behind in the battle of opinion polls. He could not help but follow the path set by Berlusconi, producing similar posters with opposing slogans.

The battle of the posters, a revival of the old media in the face of the rising importance of the Internet, marked the collective imagery of the Italian electorate in the months before the official campaign period. It was successful in building a favorable climate for Berlusconi—who continued to outdistance his competitor by four points in the polls.

The *par condicio* regulation, which had become a law (No. 28) in 2000, prevented wild media coverage (and use), but only during the month–long official campaign. As in 1996, all the televised political commercials were aired before the campaign, especially by Berlusconi's coalition who depended on the channels owned by the tycoon.

The center–left coalition, in spite of its lesser financial resources, also engaged in building and carrying out a hyper–professionalized type of campaign strategy. Abandoning the low–key style of the 1996 campaign that echoed the old tunes of the proportional era, it converted to the majoritarian logic and endeavored to choose a leader of the coalition with strong moral, political, and communication attributes. The choice fell on the former mayor of Rome, Francesco Rutelli, who had created a popular image in the eight years of his mayoralty. Nevertheless, vis–à–vis a majoritarian strategy pursued by the Olive Tree, the parties of the coalition appeared to follow disjoint communication and policy tactics, very much resembling the old pre–reform ambiguous practices. The overall image stemming from the center–left coalition was that of a fragmented and disunited bloc that was essentially punished by an electorate now accustomed to the majoritarian practice and with the bi–polarization of the political game (see Chapter Three).

Television, in the 2001 campaign, played a crucial role proving once more its overarching importance as a mega–stage for the political battle. And, of course, it was dominated—directly or indirectly, in favor or against—by Berlusconi. Thanks to his showman's savvy he succeeded in leading the game all the way through. Two tactical decisions were indeed masterful and potentially deadly for his adversary. First, Berlusconi this time refused to meet his opponent in a television "great debate," this on the presumption that by meeting an opponent he (Berlusconi) would bestow unwanted visibility on an unknown. Second, he kept a masterful *coup de theatre* that concluded his overwhelming campaign on the very last day—he appeared on RAI's most popular talk show to sign his "contract with the Italian people" in front of a national audience. In five points he illustrated the goals of his future government: reduction of taxes, defense of citizens against crime, increase of lowest social pensions to a minimum of €516 (1 million lire, widely considered to be the poverty line in Italy), creation of 1 million jobs, and the launch of great infra–structures. He solemnly promised that if, at the end of his premiership, four out of five of those commitments had not been accomplished he would withdraw from the next race.

It was perhaps the most solemn celebration of the plurality–induced personalization of Italian politics, a sort of anticipation of the new premier's plan to change Italy into a presidential republic.

Conclusion

Do the Italian political parties play the majoritarian game but look back at the old proportional system in election campaigns? Looking at the campaigns of the post–reform decade one gathers a mixed picture that may be typical of transitions. On the one side the biggest parties do not conceal their attempts to exploit the advantages of the first–past–the–post rules to consolidate their electoral power. On the other, the smaller parties, while agreeing to aggregate in coalitions, do endeavor to preserve their identities and interests while coming to terms with the coalitions (triggering a sort of proportionalization of the plurality rule) and campaign—ing on their own in the proportional districts.

The overall outcome of such a virtual (but, at times quite abrutal) tug of war is consistent with the *mixed* nature of the electoral rule introduced in Italy in 1993. As observed by Giovanni Sartori, mixed systems are likely to generate two–faced (Janus–like) parties forced to unite in the PL and to quarrel in the PR tiers (2002, p. 110).

Nevertheless, the main stream seems to flow in the direction of a stronger dominance of the PL logic and practice, much of it at the expense of proportional representation. It is the majoritarian drift that has characterized the change to the new electoral system, and was manifested over and over again by the electorate in all the elections since the reform (see Chapter Three). It was eventually espoused by a significant portion of Italian political forces, and these mostly in the conservative quarters.

The sign that it might be an unstoppable drift may be seen in the resurfaced (Summer 2003) proposal by the center–right forces (especially *Forza Italia* and the right–wing party *Alleanza Nazionale*) of a major constitutional reform leading to a presidential system or to a premiership with direct election. In either case the rationale of this proposed revolution is to strengthen government—a long–cherished dream by most Italian voters—no matter if that might entail a weakening of Parliament, and ultimately a lessening of popular representation.

The campaigning of the post–reform years shows significant cues that the majoritarian drift is presently winning over other concerns about the improvement of democratic warranties in Italy, such as those that, according to certain schools of thought, may be better offered by pure–proportional representation. Italy ex—perienced hyper–proportionalism for 40–plus years and its identification with political and government instability (and corruption) prompted a popular demand for change. Public opinion is still convinced that the old proportional system, rather than guaranteeing the representation of voters, is a life insurance for the small parties.

This is the reason why coalitions are rewarded when their campaign communication is embodied by a popular leader and shows intra–coalition cohesion. The personalization of politics and of political communication, bolstered by the media and encouraged by the PL rule, seems to epitomize the modernization of Italy's electioneering and the preferential political taste of the national electorate.

Part Three

Chapter Seven

The United States: Media Spectacle and Election 2000

by Douglas Kellner

> When the real world changes into simple images, simple images become real beings and effective motivations of a hypnotic behavior. The spectacle has a tendency to make one see the world *by means of various specialized mediations (it can no longer be grasped directly).*
> —Guy Debord

The 2000 US presidential election was one of the most bizarre and fateful in American history. Described in books as a "deadlock," "thriller," "the perfect tie," and even as "Grand Theft 2000," studies of the election have dissected its anomalies and scandals and have attempted to describe and explain what actually happened.[1] In this study I will analyze how the turn toward media politics and spectacle in US political campaigns and the curious and arguably archaic system of proportional voting in the US tilted the campaign toward George W. Bush and were prejudicial to the election of Al Gore. Gore received over 540,000 votes more than Bush, but because of the US system of proportional voting won less electoral votes and lost the crucial state of Florida. In this chapter, I will argue that media representation of the two candidates and the anomalies of the United States system of proportional representation were major factors in the highly controversial ascent to the presidency of George W. Bush. Of course, the Supreme Court decision directly decided the election results and the story of Election 2000 is highly complex and contested. Yet, focus on the media in the election and problems with the system of proportional representation provide revealing lenses on the events of the 2000 election and call attention to major problems in the US system of representational democracy.

Media spectacle and representation in election 2000

> We mortals hear only the news and know nothing at all.
> —Homer

The 2000 US presidential election, one of the closest and most hotly contested ever, was from start to finish a media spectacle. Despite predictions that the Internet was on its way to replacing television as the center of the information system, television in the 2000 US election was perhaps more influential than ever. The proliferation of television channels on cable and satellite systems multiplied political discourse and images, with several presenting round–the–clock political news and discussion. These cable news channels were organized as forms of media spectacle, with highly partisan representatives of both sides engaging opposed positions in dramatic and combative competition. The fight for ratings intensified the entertainment factor in politics, fueling the need to generate compelling political spectacle to attract audiences.

The result was unending television discussion programs with commentators lined up for the Republicans or Democrats, as hosts pretended to be neutral, but often sided with one candidate or another. Of the 24–hour cable news channels, it was clear that the Rupert Murdoch—owned Fox network was unabashedly pro–Republican, and it appeared that the NBC–owned cable networks MSNBC and CNBC were also partial toward Bush. CNN and the three major networks claimed to maintain neutrality, although major studies of television and press coverage of the election indicated that the media on the whole tended to favor Bush, as I argue below.

By all initial accounts, it would be a close election, and both sides tried to spin the media furiously, getting their "message of the day" and a positive image of their candidate on screen or into the press. Both sides provided the usual press releases and sent out e–mail messages to the major media and their supporters, which their opponents would then attempt to counter. The competing campaigns also constructed elaborate Web sites that contained their latest "messages," video clips of the candidates, and other information on the campaigns.[2] Both sides staged frequent photo opportunities, saturated the airwaves with ads, and attempted to sell their candidate to the voters.

Throughout the summer, there was not much focus on the campaigns among the public at large until the political conventions took place, where both parties traditionally gathered and produced spectacles to provide positive images of their candidate and party. The Republicans met first in Philadelphia from July 31 to August 3, filling their stage with a multi–cultural display of their supporters, leading pundits to remark that more people of color appeared on stage than were in the audience of the lily–white conservative party who had not been friendly to minorities.

The Democrats met in Los Angeles in mid–August and created carefully planned media events to show off their stars, the Clintons and the Gores, with Al and Tipper's long kiss the most circulated image of the event. For the first time, however, major television networks declared that the political party conventions were not important news stories, but were merely partisan events, and they severely cut back on primetime coverage allotted the spectacles. In particular, NBC and the Fox network broadcast baseball and entertainment shows rather than convention speeches during the early days of both conventions, and all networks cut their coverage to a minimum. CBS's Dan Rather, for instance, dismissed the conventions as "four–day infomercials"— advertisements for the parties and their candidates (CBS News, August 15).

Nonetheless, millions of people watched the conventions, and both candidates got their biggest polling boosts after their respective events, thus suggesting that the carefully contrived media displays were able to capture an audience and perhaps shape viewer perceptions of the candidates. After the conventions, no major stories emerged and not much media attention was given to the campaigns during the rest of August and September, that period leading up to the presidential debates. The Gore campaign seemed to be steadily rising in the polls while the Bush candidacy floundered.[3]

During September 2001, the relatively inexperienced George W. Bush was caught on open mike referring to a *New York Times* reporter as a "major–league asshole," with Bush's vice presidential choice, Dick Cheney, chiming in "big time." While the Bush team publicly proclaimed that it would not indulge in negative campaigning, a television ad appeared attacking Gore and the

Democrats that highlighted the phrase "RATS." Critics accused the Bush campaign of attempting to associate the vermin with DemocRATS/bureaucRATS. Bush denied that his campaign had produced this "subliminable" message (to use his own creative mispronunciation) at the same time that an ad–man working for him was bragging about it.

Moreover, as the camps haggled about debate sites and dates, it appeared that Bush was being petulant, refusing the forums suggested by the neutral debate committee and was perhaps afraid to get into the ring with the formidable Gore. Since the 1960s the presidential debates have become popular media spectacles that are often deemed crucial to the election. Hence, as the debates began in October, genuine suspense arose and significant sectors of the populace tuned in to the three events between the presidential candidates and single disputation between the competing vice presidents. Consequently, on the whole, the debates were dull, in part because host Jim Lehrer asked unimaginative questions that simply allowed the candidates to feed back their standard positions on Social Security, education, Medicare, and other issues that they had already spoken about day after day. Neither Lehrer nor others involved in the debates probed the candidates' positions or asked challenging questions on a wide range of issues from globalization and the digital divide to poverty and corporate crime that had not been addressed in the campaign. Frank Rich described the first debate in the *New York Times* as a "flop show," while Dan Rather on CBS called it "pedantic, dull, unimaginative, lackluster, humdrum, you pick the word."[4]

In Election 2000, commentators on the debates tended to grade the candidates more on their performance and style than on substance, and many believe that this strongly aided Bush. In the post–modern—image politics of the 2000 election, style became substance as both candidates endeavored to appear likable, friendly, and attractive to voters. In the presidential debates when the candidates appeared *mano a mano* to the public for the first time, not only did the media commentators focus on the form and appearance of the candidates, rather than the specific positions they took, but the networks frequently cut to "focus groups" of "undecided" voters who presented their stylistic evaluations. After the first debate, for instance, commentators noted that Gore looked "stiff" or "arrogant" while Bush appeared "likable." And after the second debate, Gore was criticized by commentators as too "passive," and then too "aggressive" after the third debate, while critics tended to let Bush off the hook.

It was, however, the spectacle of the three presidential debates and the media framing of these events that arguably provided the crucial edge for Bush.[5] At the conclusion of the first Bush–Gore debate, the initial viewer polls conducted by CBS and ABC declared Gore the winner. But the television pundits seemed to score a victory for Bush. Bob Schieffer of CBS declared, "Clearly tonight, if anyone gained from this debate, it was George Bush. He seemed to have as much of a grasp of the issues" as Gore. His colleague Gloria Borger agreed, "I think Bush did gain." CNN's Candy Crowley concluded, "They held their own, they both did.... In the end, that has to favor Bush, at least with those who felt . . .he's not ready for prime time."

Even more helpful to Bush was the focus on Gore's debate performance. Gore was criticized for his sighs and style (a "bully," declared ABC's Sam Donaldson) and was savaged for alleged misstatements. The Republicans immediately spun that Gore had "lied" when he told a story of a young Florida girl forced to stand in class because of a shortage of desks. The school principal of the locale in question denied this, but the media had a field day, with a Murdoch–owned *New York Post* boldface headline trumpeting "LIAR! LIAR!" Subsequent interviews indicated that the girl *did* have to stand and that there *was* a desk shortage, and testimony from her father and a picture confirmed this, but the spin was on that Gore was a "liar." Moreover, Gore had misspoken during the first debate in a story illustrating his work in making the Federal Emergency Management Administration (FEMA) more efficient, claiming that he had visited Texas with its director after a recent hurricane. As it turns out, although Gore had played a major role in improving FEMA and had frequently traveled with its director to crisis sites, and while he had been to Texas after the hurricane, the fact that he had not accompanied the director in the case cited accelerated claims that Gore was a "serial exaggerator," or even liar, who could not be trusted.

This Republican mantra was repeated throughout the rest of the campaign, and whereas the press piled on Gore every time there was a minor misstatement, critics argued that Bush was able to get away with whoppers in the debate and on the campaign trail on substantial issues.[6] For example, when he claimed in a debate with Gore that he was for a "patients' bill of rights" that would allow patients to sue their HMOs for malpractice, in fact, Bush had blocked such policies in Texas and opposed a bill in Congress that would allow patients the right to sue. And few critics skewered Bush over the misstatement in the second debate, delivered with a highly inappropriate smirk, that the three racists who had brutally killed a black man in Texas were going to be executed. In fact, one had testified against the others and had been given a life sentence in exchange; moreover, because all cases were under appeal it was simply wrong for the governor to claim that they were going to be executed, since this undercut their right of appeal. The media also had given Bush a pass on the record number of executions performed under his reign in Texas, the lax review procedures, and the large number of contested executions where there were questions of mental competence, proper legal procedures, and even evidence that raised doubts about Bush's execution of specific prisoners.

Thus, although a fierce debate over prescription drugs in the first debate led to allegations by Gore that Bush was misrepresenting his own prescription drug plan, driving Bush to verbally assault Gore, the media did not bother to look and see that Bush *had* misrepresented his plan. Nor did many note that Gore was correct, despite Bush's impassioned denials, that seniors earning more than $25,000 a year would get no help from Bush's plan for four or five years. Moreover, after the third and arguably decisive presidential debate, the MSNBC commentators and punditry were heavily weighted toward pro–Bush voices. In questioning Republican vice–presidential candidate Dick Cheney about the third debate, Chris Matthews lobbed an easy question to him attacking Al Gore; moments later when Democratic House Majority Leader Dick Gephardt came on, once again Matthews assailed Gore in his question! Pollster Frank Luntz presented a focus group of "undecided" voters, the majority of which had switched to Bush during the debate and who uttered primarily anti–Gore sentiments when interviewed (MSNBC forgot to mention that Luntz is a Republican activist). Former Republican Senator Alan Simpson was allowed to throw barbs at Gore, to the delight and assent of host Brian Williams, while there was no

Democrat allowed to counter the Republican in this segment. The pundits, including Matthews, former Reagan–Bush speechwriter and professional Republican ideologue Peggy Noonan, and accused plagiarist Mike Barnacle, all uttered pro–Bush messages, while the two more liberal pundits provided more balanced analysis of the pros and cons of both sides in the debate, rather than just spin for Bush.

Gore was on the defensive for several weeks after the debates, and Bush's polls steadily rose.[7] Moreover, the tremendous amount of coverage of the polls no doubt helped Bush. While Gore had been rising in the polls from his convention up until the debates, occasionally experiencing a healthy lead, the polls were favorable to Bush from the conclusion of the first debate until the election. Almost every night, the television news opened with the polls, which usually showed Bush ahead, sometimes by 10 points or more. As the election night results would show, these polls were off the mark but they became *the* story of the election as the November 7 vote approached.

The polls were indeed one of the scandals of what some felt was shameful media coverage of the campaign. Arianna Huffington mentioned in a November 2, 2000, syndicated column that on a CNN/USA Today/Gallup poll released at 6:23 p.m. on Friday, October 27, George W. Bush was proclaimed to hold a 13 point lead over Al Gore; in a CNN/Time poll released around two hours later that night at 8:36 p.m., Bush's lead was calculated to be 6 points. When Huffington called the CNN polling director, he declared that the wildly divergent polls were "statistically in agreement . . . given the polls' margin of sampling error." The polling director explained that with a margin of error of 3.5 percent, either candidate's support could be 3.5 percent higher or lower, indicating that a spread of as much as 20 points could qualify as "statistically in agreement," thus admitting that the polls do not really signify much of anything, as in fact election night results showed.

The polls were thus highly problematic during the 2000 campaign. Poll fatigue had set in with the public, and, as Huffington noted in her syndicated column cited above, the major polling organizations admitted that they were getting a less than 50 percent response rate. Moreover, the national polls were irrelevant, because in an Electoral College system, it is the number of states won that is the key to victory, and not national polling figures. In fact, the Electoral College system, in which the candidate who gets the most votes in a state wins the state and the candidate who wins the most states wins the election, would come under attack during the intense Battle for the White House in the Florida Recount Wars. For Gore won more than half a million more votes than Bush, many states that were very close were won by Bush, so a more proportional voting system would better reflect the will of the people, as many reformers argued.[8]

Despite all their flaws, network news coverage focused on the polls, or the strategies, mechanics, and ups and downs of the campaigns, rather than the key issues or the public's real concerns. With a declining amount of news coverage on the major network news, and sound bites in which news and information were condensed into even smaller fragments, media focus on the horse race and strategic dimension of the presidential campaigns meant that less and less time would be devoted to discussion of issues, the candidates, and the stakes of the election.

In this environment, the campaigns sought to create positive images of their candidates through daily photo opportunities and television ads, thus contributing to intensification of a superficial politics of the image. The television ads presented positive spectacles of the candidates' virtues and negative representations of their opponents' flaws. Contested states such as Florida were saturated with wall–to–wall advertising, and consequently Election 2000 campaign costs were the highest in history in which a record $3 billion was dispersed. The ads were closely scrutinized for distortion, exaggerations, and lies, with Internet Webzines such as *Slate.com* and some television networks providing regular analysis of the ads, while replaying and closely analyzing the more controversial ones.[9]

Both candidates ran intense phone campaigns. Republican voters could be thrilled to get a pre–recorded call from George W. Bush himself, telling them that he wanted their votes. On the Democratic side, there was a late campaign barrage of pre–recorded telephone calls to black voters from Bill Clinton, while Ed Asner recorded a call to be sent to seniors in Florida warning them about Bush's Social Security program. Of course, Hollywood celebrities and rock stars also campaigned for the candidates. Gore used his Harvard roommate Tommy Lee Jones, *West Wing*

President Martin Sheen, and an array of young Hollywood stars to campaign for him, while Bush used Bo Derek and members of the Hollywood right such as Bruce Willis.

Yet it was perhaps late–night comics and *Saturday Night Live*, the longtime satirical NBC show, that most pungently exemplified the continued importance of television to electoral politics and that also made clear that contemporary US politics is media spectacle. The comics had a field day satirizing the know–nothing smiling papa's boy "Dubya" (aka W., or Shrub, the little Bush) and Al Gore, the stiff and pompous senator from Tennessee. Likewise, *Saturday Night Live* ridiculed the candidates after the debates in segments that were widely circulated and repeated frequently on nightly news as well as on a pre–election special, giving rise to the claim that the *SNL* piece was the "most important political writing of the year."[10]

The *Saturday Night Live* satire symmetrized Bush and Gore as dim light bulbs, who were equally ludicrous. The presentations of Gore in particular were arguably inaccurate and defamatory, depicting the intelligent and articulate vice president and author as slow talking, clichéd, and bumbling. It is true that Gore tended to dumb down his discourse for the debates and repeated certain phrases to make key points, but the satire arguably distorted his speech patterns and mannerisms, which were nowhere near as slow and lumbering as in the satire. These often–repeated satires were perhaps as important as Republican attack ads in creating a negative public image of Gore. Their constant reiteration on the NBC news channels provided not only advertisements for the popular Saturday night television show, but unpaid attack ads for the Republicans.

Bush's turnaround in the polls in October after his numbers had been steadily dipping for weeks was seemingly boosted by what was perceived as his successful appearance on the debates and on popular talk shows, such as *Oprah*, where an image of the much–beloved African American talk hostess giving him a smooch was widely circulated. Some claimed that the talk shows were a natural for the more relaxed Bush, although there were debates over whether his appearance on *Late Show with David Letterman* hurt or helped his efforts, as he appeared giddy and was unable to answer effectively the tough questions Letterman posed.

In any case, both candidates made appearances on the major late–night talk shows, as well as other popular television venues previously off–limits to presidential candidates. In general, television spectacle helps to boost the chances of the most telegenic candidate, and according to media commentary, Bush repeatedly scored high in ratings in "the likeability factor." Polls continued to present Bush as more popular than Al Gore, and most media commentators predicted that he would win the election handily.[11]

Media bias in the representations of Bush and Gore

> You've heard Al Gore say he invented the Internet. Well, if he was so smart, why do all the addresses begin with "W"?
> —George W. Bush

In the post–modern politics of promotion, candidates are packaged as commodities, marketed as a brand name, and sold as a bill of goods. In a presidential race, campaigns are dominated by image consultants, advertising mavens, spin doctors, and political operatives who concoct daily photo opportunities to make the campaign look appealing, "messages" sound attractive, and "events" present the candidates in an attractive format. Such campaigns are, of course, expensive and require tremendous budgets that make competing impossible for candidates without access to the mega–fortunes needed to run a media politics campaign. In turn, such mega–spectacles render politicians beholden to those who cough up the massive amount of dollars to pay for the extravaganzas and the vast apparatus of producers, spinners, and operatives to create them.

Bush's brand name was his family trademark, son of the former president and Bush dynasty heir apparent, with his own distinctive "compassionate conservatism." The latter phrase shows the bogus and spurious nature of presidential packaging, as there is little "compassion" in the record of the Texas governor who executed a record number of prison inmates, who cut welfare lists and social programs, and who promised more of the same on the national level.[12] In the politics of presidential marketing, however, creation of image takes precedence over ideas, style replaces substance, and presentation trumps policy. With politics becoming a branch of marketing, the more marketable candidate is easier to sell. Thus, it is not surprising that Bush's image, style, and presentation trumped Gore's ideas, experience, and policies with large segments of the public.

Bush had another major asset in the competition for votes and marketing of the candidates. Cultural historians make distinctions between "character," based on one's moral fiber and history of behavior, and "personality," which has to do with how one presents oneself to others.[13] The new culture of personality emphasizes charm, likability, attractiveness, and the ability to present oneself in positive images. Bush was clearly Mr. Personality, instantly likable, a hale–fellow–well–met and friendly glad–hander who was able to charm audiences. He was becoming a media celebrity whose qualifications to be president were rarely probed by the mainstream corporate media, but he was able to play effectively the "presidential contender" and provide a resonant personality. Moreover, Bush was able to transmit his likable qualities via television, whereas Gore frequently had more difficulty in coming across as personable and translating his considerable intelligence and experience into easily consumable sound–bites and images.[14]

The Texas governor, who was to many more of a figure of personality than character, was also able to turn the "character issue"—with the complicity of the press—against Gore and convince audiences that he, George W. Bush, was a man of "character" as well as personality. The Bush camp used the term "character" as a code word to remind audiences of the moral lapses of Bill Clinton and of Gore's association with the president, in a sustained collapse of one into the other. The Bush campaign also systematically attacked Gore's character and credibility, and the media bought into this (see Kellner, 2001; Jamieson and Waldman, 2003; and Altermann, 2003).

Furthermore, Bush, more than the deadly serious and policy–oriented Gore (demeaned as a "wonk" by many), was entertaining; he was amusing and affable in debates, even if not commanding in argumentation and substantive position. Like Ronald Reagan, Bush looked good on the run, with a friendly smile and wave, and in general seemed able to banter and connect with his audiences better than Gore. Bush's misstatements and errors were amusing, and on late–night talk shows he poked fun at himself for his mispronunciations and gaffes; *Slate.com* compiled a list of "Bushisms," and they were as entertaining as David Letterman's *Top Ten List* and Jay Leno's nightly NBC monologue, which often made jokes about Gore and Bush.

Moreover, large sectors of the media despised Gore and tended to like Bush. As Eric Alterman notes:

> the intensity of the media's anti–Gore obsession is a bit bizarre, but even more so, given the strictures of journalistic objectivity, is the lack of compunction they feel about openly demonstrating it. At an early New Hampshire debate between Gore and Bill Bradley, reporters openly booed him, "objectivity" be damned. "The 300 media types watching in the press room at Dartmouth were, to use the appropriate technical term, totally grossed out," *Time* reported. "Whenever Gore came on too strong, the room erupted in a collective jeer, like a gang of fifteen–year–old Heathers cutting down some hapless nerd."
>
> *Washington Post* White House reporter Dana Milbank offers this reasoned, mature explanation: Gore is sanctimonious, and that's sort of the worst thing you can be in the eyes of the press. And he has been disliked all along, and it was because he gives a sense that he's better than us—he's better than everybody, for that matter, but the sense that he's better than us as reporters. Whereas President Bush probably is sure that he's better than us—he's probably right, but he does not convey that sense. He does not seem to be dripping with contempt when he looks at us, and I think that has something to do with the coverage.
>
> Bill Keller, who almost became executive editor of the *New York Times*, was no less scholarly than Milbank, but like any good pundit, multiplied his own resentments by fifty million. "One big reason 50 million voters went instead for an apparent lightweight they didn't entirely trust was that they didn't want to have Al Gore in their living rooms for four years," Keller wrote on the paper's Op–Ed page. Included in his argument was the behavior of his three–year–old, who, during the 2000 campaign, "went around chanting the refrain: 'Al Gore is a snore.'" Imagine where she might have learned to do that!
>
> During the 2000 election, both the *Times* and the *Post* assigned reporters to Gore who hated his guts and so repeatedly misled their readers. Katharine Seelye's and Ceci Connolly's coverage turned out to be so egregious that the two were singled out by the conservative *Financial Times of London* as "hostile to the [Gore] campaign," unable to hide their "contempt for the candidate." (And don't get me started on the topic of "Panchito" Bruni's daily valentines to George W. during this period, carried on page one of the Paper of Record, i.e. The *New York Times*.)[15]

The American public seems to like entertaining and interesting politicians and politics and to sometimes resent media critiques of politicians they like. Hence, when stories broke a few days before the election that Bush had been arrested 20 years before on a DWI charge and had since covered this over and even lied about it, the populace and polls did not punish him. When asked of highs and lows of the campaign on election night, Bush said with his trademark smirk that even the lows "turned out to be good for us," alluding to polls that indicate that Bush got a rise in popularity after revelations of his drunk driving charge. As with Clinton's survival of his sex scandals and the Republican impeachment campaign, it seems as if the public empathizes with the politicians' foibles and resents moral indictments of at least those with whom voters sympathize. Obviously, Clinton was a highly empathetic personality whom voters could sympathize with, and many resented the Republican moral crusade against him. Similarly, voters liked Bush and seemed not to be affected by the embarrassing disclosure of his DWI record and its longtime cover-up.[16]

Talk radio was an important medium during the campaign, just as it had been over the last decade in US politics. It was the relatively new form of unrestrained talk radio that first mobilized conservatives against Bill Clinton after his election in 1992, providing a basis of indignation and anger that fueled the circulation of the details of the Clinton sex scandal and generated support for his impeachment. Of course, the very excesses of right–wing talk radio provided a backlash, and some stations chose liberals to counter the conservative hosts, but most liberal programs were soon cancelled and by 2000 right–wing hosts completely dominated talk radio.

Indeed, during Election 2000 and the ensuing struggle for the presidency, right–wing talk radio had a comeback, energizing its old audience and finding new ones, while projecting the hatred of Clinton onto Gore. The narcissistic and demagogic Rush Limbaugh, who had mercifully been taken off television because of declining ratings and who had seemed to disappear from the front–stage of national mainstream media, reappeared in all his virulent unglory, frequently appearing on NBC channels, which rehabilitated the discredited demagogue to celebrity and credibility. Limbaugh and other right–wing blowhards grew louder and more aggressive than ever, demonizing Gore and mobilizing conservative constituents to vote for Bush, helping as well to organize against the Democrat candidate once the post–election struggle for the presidency erupted.

Moreover, and importantly, major research studies of the nexus between media and politics revealed that both the broadcast media and the press were pro–Bush and that this bias perhaps won the Republican enough votes ultimately to wrest the election victory from Gore and the Democrats (although, of course, many maintain that the election was stolen and that Gore had won the plurality of Electoral College votes, as well as the popular vote). A study by the Pew Research Center and the Project for Excellence in Journalism (PEJ) examined 2,400 newspaper, television, and Internet stories in five different weeks between February and June 2000, and indicated that 76 percent of the coverage included one of two themes: that Gore lies and exaggerates or is marred by scandal. The most common theme about Bush, the study found, is that he is a "different kind of Republican." A follow–up PEJ report concluded:

> In the culminating weeks of the 2000 presidential race, the press coverage was strikingly negative, and Vice President Al Gore has gotten the worst of it, according to a new study released today by the Committee of Concerned Journalists.
>
> Gore's coverage was decidedly more negative, more focused on the internal politics of campaigning and had less to do with citizens than did his Republican rival.
>
> In contrast, George W. Bush was twice as likely as Gore to get coverage that was positive in tone. Coverage of the governor was also more issue–oriented and more likely to be directly connected to citizens.
>
> These are some of the key findings of a major new study of press coverage in newspapers, television and on the Internet during key weeks in September and October.[17]

Hence, the early coding of Gore in the mainstream media was that he tended to exaggerate and even lie and was implicated in many scandals in the Clinton administration, while the media bought the Bush line that he was a different type of Republican, a "compassionate conservative" and "a reformer with results" who worked with Democrats and Republicans in Texas "to get things done." When the election would heat up in the fall, the Bush campaign would exploit these motifs, and the mainstream media would generally go along with this line, without serious investigation of Bush's record or his own exaggerations and misstatements.[18]

One of the most utilized examples of Gore the liar and "serial exaggerator" was the alleged claim that he had invented the Internet. In fact, Gore had made no such claim, although the media, the Republican spinners, and Bush himself constantly referred to this urban myth. Bush burst out in one of the debates that "his opponent" claimed to "have invented the Internet" and then smirked in contempt and during the election often repeated the joke, caught many times in news footage: "You've heard Al Gore say he invented the Internet. Well, if he was so smart, why do all the addresses begin with `W'?"

This lie about Gore, and Bush's systematic exploitation of the myth, speaks volumes about the quality of the Bush campaign and media complicity in its spin. First, it is simply untrue that Gore claimed he "invented" the Internet.[19] Second, it is interesting how Bush and his handlers utilized the "W" as a trademark to distinguish Bush from his father and how Bush became popularly identified as W., or the Texas–inflected "Dubya." Whereas JFK's initials were an apt summary of his style and achievements, and LBJ earned the gravity of his initials through many years in the Senate, culminating in becoming Senate Majority leader, then gaining the vice presidency and presidency, George W. Bush was popularly referred to as "W.," an empty signifier that really didn't stand for anything in particular, although had the media probed the infamous initial they would have discovered a truly spectacular story.

In fact, the "W" in Bush Junior's name referred to Herbert Walker, the father of the woman, Dorothy Walker, who George W. Bush's grandfather, Prescott Bush, married (the H.W. in Bush senior's name referred to Herbert Walker, pointing to the largely unknown origins of Bush family power and money). While the mainstream media investigated and widely discussed any slightly scandalous aspect of Gore family history, they neglected the much more colorful Bush family history. For example, Prescott Bush managed the bank that helped fund Hitler and the Nazis, while Herbert Walker, Prescott Bush's close business associate, helped run businesses for Stalin's Russia and Mussolini's Italy, as well as Hitler's Germany.[20] One of the scandals of Election 2000 is that the press did not delve into Bush family history and its unsavory connections and activities, but largely focused on the day–to–day campaign activities and daily spins of the candidates, how they were faring in the polls, and the personalities of the candidates.

Bush's appeal was predicated on his being "just folks," a "good guy," like "you and me." Thus, his anti–intellectualism and lack of intellectual gravity, exhibited every time he opened his mouth and mangled the English language, helped promote voter identification. As a sometime Republican speechwriter Doug Gamble once mused, "Bush's shallow intellect perfectly reflects an increasingly dumbed–down America. To many Americans Bush is `just like us,' a Fox–television President for a Fox–television society."[21]

The media rarely challenged Bush who seemed to have not only charmed large sectors of the American public, but was effective in schmoozing the media. Another survey released of press coverage after the conventions showed a decisive partiality for Bush. The Center for Media and Public Affairs (CMPA) study of television election news coverage before, during, and after the conventions (released on August 14) concluded, "Network evening news coverage of the GOP convention was more favorable toward George W. Bush, while Al Gore received mostly unfavorable television references, according to a new study released by the CMPA." The study also found that "Bush has received more favorable coverage than Gore throughout the 2000 campaign, reversing a trend that favored Bill Clinton over his GOP opponents in 1992 and 1996."[22]

Surprisingly perhaps, Bush fared as well with the print media and establishment press as with television. Supporting the studies of pro–Bush bias, Charlie Peters reported in the Washington Monthly that according to the PEJ studies, the *New York Times* front page "carried nine anti–Gore articles and six anti–Bush; 12 pro–Gore and 21 pro–Bush" (November 2000). Howard Kurtz, media critic of the *Washington Post*, reported: "Those who believe the media were easier on Bush will find some support in a new Project for Excellence in Journalism study. Examining television, newspaper, and Internet coverage from the last week in September through the third week in October, the report says Bush got nearly twice as many stories as Gore" (November 6, 2000). Moreover, only one in ten of the pieces analyzed the candidates' policy differences, with two thirds focusing on the candidates' performance, strategy, or tactics. 24 percent of the

Bush stories were positive, compared to 13 percent for Gore, while the Bush stories focused more on issues than character or campaign strategy.

A German group, Media Tenor, also documented a persistent anti–Gore and pro–Bush bias in mainstream media presentation of the candidates.[23] Thus, three different research projects found strong media bias in the election coverage. To be sure, such "positive" and "negative" scoring of images and discourses is difficult, debatable, and not always completely accurate, but I would argue that even more significant than alleged bias in new stories in the mainstream media is the preponderance of conservative punditry and, even more significant, the exclusion of widespread media documentation and discussion of key aspects of George W. Bush's life, record in business and government, and obvious lack of qualifications for the presidency.

In his 1992 book *Fooling America*, Robert Parry documents the pack journalism of the mainstream media in the 1980s and 1990s, arguing that the horde follows "conventional wisdom," recycling the dominant and predictable opinions, while failing to pursue stories or develop positions outside of or against the prevailing views of the day. During Campaign 2000, journalists on the whole tended to accept the line of the Bush campaign concerning Gore's purported negatives while promoting the view that the Bush camp advanced that Bush was a uniter, not a divider, a "compassionate conservative," and someone who pursued "bipartisan" politics in order "to get things done."

Clearly, media pundits tended to favor Bush over Gore. As Eric Alterman demonstrated in *Sound and Fury: The Making of the Punditocracy* (revised, 2000), conservatives had trained a cadre of media commentators, well versed in the art of sound bite and staying on message, and there were many, many more conservatives than liberals on the airwaves. The conservative punditocracy trashed Gore daily, while Bush escaped critical scrutiny of his record in Texas, his limited experience, his problematic proposals, and his almost daily misstatements. The conservative pundits, however, aggressively promoted the Republican message of the day and served as ubiquitous shock troops for the Bush machine.

The bias in the mainstream media favoritism toward Bush not only came through in how the media presented and framed the two opposing candidates, but in how they failed to pursue George W. Bush's family history, scandalous business career, dubious record as governor, lack of qualifications for the presidency, and serious character flaws. None of the many newspaper, magazine, and television reports on the Bush and Gore family history mentioned the reports on the origins of the Bush dynasty fortune in a bank that financed German fascism or pursued the Bush family financial scandals that continued through Jeb, Neil, and George W. Bush.[24]

There was no probing of the Bush family involvement during Election 2000 in the savings and loan (S&L) scandal, arguably one of the biggest financial debacles in US' history, costing taxpayers over half a trillion dollars to bail out the failed S&L institutions which had gone on a spending orgy after deregulation in the early 1980s. George H. W. Bush and James Baker were instrumental in the deregulation of the industry during the Reagan administration, and their families and friends had bought up and looted S&Ls, including the Silverado S&L scandal involving Neil Bush (see Brewton, 1992).

There was also little coverage of the political scandals that Bush senior had been involved in, such as the Iran–Contra scandal, the US arming of Saddam Hussein, or the misdeeds of the CIA under Bush's directorship (see Kellner, 1990, 1992; Parry, 1992). In addition, there was almost no reporting on George W. Bush's personal or financial history, which included reports of using favoritism to get out of military service and then going AWOL, failing to complete his military reserve service. There was little discussion of his checkered business career, including allegations that his father's friends bailed out his failing oil industry and that he then unloaded his own stock in the Harken energy company that had bailed him out, selling before revelations of a bad financial report and failing to report the sale to the Securities and Exchange Commission, giving rise to charges of "insider trading." Bush's poor record as Texas governor was also not probed, nor was his personal failings and inexperience that should have disqualified him from serving as president.

Books, articles, and easily accessible Internet sites document the entire scandalous history of George W. Bush and his dubious dynasty, but lazy and incompetent functionaries of the mainstream media failed to probe this rich mine of material and scandals—whereas there were few embarrassments or negative aspects of Al Gore's past that were not mined and endlessly discussed on talk radio and among conservative television punditry. Likewise, there were few in–depth discussions of the record of Bush's vice–presidential choice Dick Cheney, the major role he would play in a Bush White House, and his precarious health. Cheney had one of the most hard–right voting records in Congress and was heavily involved in the oil industry as CEO of Halliburton industries, one of the worst polluters and most ruthless corporations in an industry known for its hardball Robber Barons.[25]

Bush thus benefited significantly from media coverage of Election 2000; major empirical and journalistic studies suggest that the media was heavily prejudiced in his favor and I have argued that Bush also benefited by the domination of conservative punditry and failure to investigate adequately his history, record and qualifications, the scandals that his family has been involved in, and the record of his running mate Dick Cheney, one of the most hard–right political operatives of the present era. There had been little investigative reporting on Bush and a preponderance of favorable stories for Bush and unfavorable ones for Gore, as evidenced in the CMPA, PEW, and Media Tenor studies cited above. Likewise, television pundits seemed to favor Bush over Gore. Media critic David Corn noted that commentators such as John McLaughlin, Mary Matalin, Peggy Noonan, and many of the Sunday network talk–show hosts prophesized a sizable Bush victory and tended to favor the Texas governor.[26]

Yet the election was the closest in history and election night and the aftermath comprised one of the most enthralling and gripping media spectacles in recent history. Despite the drama of the election and its highly contested aftermath, however, there was little self–criticism of the role of the media in Election 2000 visible in the mainstream media and with the September 11 terror attacks discussion of electoral problems was off the agenda. While there were efforts to reform election finances and voting technology, there were no significant reforms of the US electoral system that appeared to be dysfunctional in Election 2000 with arguable malfunctioning of the media, voter technology, and the democratic system itself (see Kellner, 2001). Discussion of Electoral College reform disappeared and no commissions studied the flaws in the US' voting system that made possible the problems of Election 2000. Yet the election called attention limitations of the US' system of democracy and demands sustained reflections on the importance of reforms to revitalize democracy in the United States.

The Electoral College and proportional voting

A popular government without popular information, or the means of acquiring it, is but a prologue to a farce or a tragedy, or perhaps both.
—James Madison

The confusion and dysfunctionality evident in Election 2000 reveal problems with the arguably outmoded and dangerously undemocratic Electoral College system and the problematical nature of the US' system of proportional voting. Many were surprised to learn that the Electoral College involved a system whereby those chosen to vote in the ritual in which the president was chosen did not necessarily have to follow the mandate of the voters in their district. In practice, state legislatures began binding electors to the popular vote, although as was abundantly clear in Election 2000, "faithless electors," electors who vote for whomever they please, were theoretically possible (half of the states attempt to legally bind electors to the choice of voters in their state, but it would still be possible to shift one's vote, an intolerable outcome for a genuinely democratic society and a possibility much discussed in Election 2000). Direct election of senators, in fact, required a constitutional amendment in 1913 because election of the US Senate also originally operated with the mediation of electors who choose senators, rather than through direct voting by the people, which is now the case and which many argued should also be the model for presidential elections. This reform would call for a direct election for the president, without the mediation of electors, as is the case with the House and the Senate.

The current Electoral College system, as critics have maintained, is based on eighteenth–century concerns and is arguably obsolete and in need of systematic reconstruction in the twenty–first century. Initially, the Electoral College was part of a compromise between state and local government. Allowing electors to choose the president provided guarantees to more conservative politicians who wanted the Electoral College to serve as a buffer between what they perceived as an unruly and potentially dangerous mob and the more educated and civic–minded legislators, who could, if they wished, overturn actual votes by the people.

Moreover, the proportional representation system in the Electoral College has serious problems that have come out in the heated debates over Election 2000. Smaller states are disproportionately awarded with Electoral College votes, so that voters in less populated states such as Idaho or Wyoming have more proportionate influence in choosing the president than in states such as California or New York. As Duke University's Alex Keyssar argued in a November 20, 2000 *New York Times* Op–Ed piece,

> disproportionate weighting of the votes of smaller states violates the principle of one person, one vote that most of us believe in and that, according to a series of Supreme Court decisions in the 1960s, lies at the heart of our democracy. "To say that a vote is worth more in one district than in another would . . . run counter of our fundamental ideas of democratic government," the court announced in 1964. "Legislators," wrote Chief Justice Earl Warren, "represent people, not trees or acres." Yet 18 million people in New York now get 33 electoral votes for the presidency while fewer than 14 million people in a collection of small states also get 33.

Thus, the current system of proportionate state votes where all states get two votes and then the rest are divided according to population is unfair; for example, as Jim Hightower notes, Wyoming's electors and proportionate vote represent 71,000 voters each, whereas Florida's electors each represent 238,000.[27] A more reasonable system would simply allot states proportionate votes according to their populations, so that each vote throughout the nation would be equal in choosing a president. Further problems with the US Electoral College and system of propor-tional representation involve the winner–takes–all rule operative in most states. As the Florida battle illustrates, in a winner–takes–all system 100 percent representation could go to a 50.1 percent majority in state presidential elections (or less if there were more than two candidates, as is increasingly the case in presidential elections). Maine and Nebraska are exceptions, and it would be possible to follow their example and to split presidential state votes proportionately according to the actual percentage of votes candidates get in each separate state, rather than following the winner–takes–all rule, where a handful of votes in a state such as Florida gives the entire state, and even the election, to one candidate.

Hence, the Electoral College and US system of proportional representation should be seriously debated and reforms should be undertaken if US democracy is to revitalize itself in the new millennium after its most scandalous debacle. As many have argued, there are strong reasons for proportionate representation in US presidential elections,[28] but it arguably should be without electors and with the public directly electing the president in a more proportionately fair and just electoral system, as opposed to a winner–takes–all state vote and subsequent ratification by electors. "Electors" are rather mysteriously chosen in any case and could potentially be "faithless" and vote for a candidate not chosen by their state. Other options would be a winner–takes–all national popular vote, but this would seem to contradict the desire to have a balance of power among the states and to ascribe the states a significant political role, as was envisaged in the original Constitution of the United States. On the other hand, any number of reforms to the current system could be proposed and should be seriously discussed.

Indeed, for US democracy to work in the new millennium, it should appoint high–level commissions to study how to modernize and update the system of electing the president. Since the political establishment cannot be counted upon to undertake these reforms, it will be necessary for publics—academic, local, and national—to devise reforms for the seriously challenged system of "democracy" in the United States. Furthermore, it is clear that money has corrupted the current electoral system and that finance reform is necessary to avoid continued corruption by lobbies, corporations, and the influence purchasing and peddling that a campaign system fueled by mega bucks produces. The current election system financing scheme and millions of dollars needed for a federal election ensure that only candidates from the two major parties have a chance of winning, that only candidates who are able to raise millions of dollars can run, and that those who do run and win are beholden to those who have financed their campaigns—guaranteeing control of the political system by corporations and the wealthy.

In Election 2000, the excessive amount of money pumped into the $3 billion–plus electoral campaigns guaranteed that neither candidate would say anything to offend the moneyed interests funding the election, assuring that both parties would pitch their campaigns to the middle, avoid controversy, and thus avoid key issues of importance and concern. The ways that expensive campaigns indebted the two major parties to their contributors were obvious in the initial appointments made by the Cheney–Bush transition team, which rewarded precisely those sectors and corporations who most heartily supported the Bush dynasty presidency. Moreover, the Bush administration provided legislative awards for its major contributors, allowed the big corporations that supported them to write Bush administration energy policy, communication policy, and to help draft legislation for deregulation and new laws that served their interests, in effect allowing big contributors to make public policy (see Kellner, 2001, 187, ff).

The Clinton administration was also notorious in its fund–raising activities, which it maintained were necessary to compete with Republicans in highly expensive election campaigns. In this situation, the only way to curtail blatant and growing corruption in allowing major contributors to shape public policy is to have dramatic election campaign reform. In 2001, a McCain–Feingold finance reform bill was passed, but it has been continually watered down and is unlikely to reform political funding.

Moreover, there is a strong case to go further and argue for public financing of elections. Four states currently allow full public financing for candidates who agree to campaign fund–raising and spending limits (Arizona, Maine, Massachusetts, and Vermont), and this would be a splendid model for the entire nation. Public financing for elections at local, state, and national levels would only be viable in a media era with free national television, free access to local media, and Internet sites offered to the candidates. Indeed, the television networks should also be required to provide free airtime to presidential candidates to make their pitches, and television–paid political advertising should be eliminated (see the elaboration of this argument in Kellner 1990). The broadcasting networks were given a tremendous bonanza when the Federal Communications Commission (FCC) provided a wealth of spectrum to use for digital broadcasting, doubling the amount of spectrum space it licensed to television broadcasters with estimates of the value of the space ranging up to $70 billion. Congress failed to establish public service requirements that used to be in place before the Reagan–Bush–Clinton deregulation of telecommunications and as a fair payback for the broadcast spectrum giveaway, broadcasting institutions should provide free time for political discourse that strengthens democracy.

To be sure, efforts were made and defeated to get the television networks to provide resources that would enable the public to get messages from the candidates, clearly presenting their positions. President Clinton appointed an advisory panel to assess how to update public service requirements of television broadcasts in the wake of the spectrum giveaway. The panel recommended that television broadcasters voluntarily offer five minutes of candidate–centered airtime in the thirty days before the election. Clinton proposed this recommendation in his 1998 State of the Union address, but broadcasters fiercely rejected the proposal, and in the Senate, John McCain and Conrad Burns announced that they would legislatively block the FCC's free airtime initiative. In fact, political advertising is a major cash cow for the television networks who regularly charge political candidates excessively high rates, although they are supposed to allow "lowest unit charge" (LUC) for political advertising. Such LUC rates, however, mean that the ads could be preempted, and desperate campaigns want to make sure that they get their advertising message out at a crucial time and thus are forced to pay higher rates.[29]

Obviously, campaign finance reform should require taking a hard look at the role of television advertising and serious consideration of the providing of free television time to major political candidates. A fair election requires that candidates be able to present their ideas to the public and to have a chance to respond to their opponent's criticisms, whether via television ads, interviews, or televised speeches. The current situation of the necessity of high–priced ads in a presidential campaign requires record levels of fund–raising and ensures that money will corrupt the political process.

There is little doubt that US democracy is in serious crisis, and unless there are serious reforms, its decline will accelerate. Although electoral participation increased from an all–time low in 1996 of 49 percent of the eligible electorate to 51 percent in Election 2000, this percentage is still extremely low, putting the United States near the bottom of democratic participation in presidential elections. Obviously, about half of the country is alienated from electoral politics and the centrist campaigns of both sides in Election 2000, geared toward a mythical center and suburban swing voters and governed by polls and focus groups, were not likely to inspire voters and bring them into the political process. Thus, US democracy remains in crisis and there will probably be no significant reforms until a critical mass of people see the flaws of the US system and demand democratic reform.

Notes:`

[1] This study draws upon and expands arguments set out in *Grand Theft 2000* (Kellner, 2001) and draws upon the major books on Election 2000 including Tapper, 2001; Bugliosi, 2001; Dershowitz, 2001; Schechter, 2001; Greenfield, 2001; Miller, 2001; Milbank, 2001; the *Washington Post*, 2001; the *New York Times*, 2001; Simon, 2001; Ceaser and Busch, 2001; Nichols, 2001; Toobin, 2001; Bruni, 2002; and Sabato, 2002.

[2] In an excellent overview of the role of Internet sites in Election 2000 and issues involved in online politics, see Stephen Coleman, "What Was New? Online Innovation in the 2000 Elections," in Schechter, 2001: 120–33.

[3] See the daily commentary on the campaign in Howard Kurtz's media columns archived at http://www.washingtonpost.com (30 December, 2003); Millbank, 2001: 307ff; and Bruni, 2002: 163ff.

[4] The following analysis is based on videotapes I made of the election and analysis in Kellner, 2001. Pundit quotes and analysis of the first debate are found in Howard Kurtz, *Washington Post* (4 October, 2000).

[5] See Ceaser and Busch who argue that: "Everything turned around for George Bush during the period of the debates.... It was the cumulative effect of the three debates themselves that carried him past the vice-president and into a modest lead that lasted until the final weekend" (2001: 148–150). My argument is that it was the framing of the debate by the media that was decisive (Kellner, 2001: 13ff; see a similar analysis in Altermann (2003: 160ff) who provides further examples of how the media framed the debates in ways positive toward Bush and negatively toward Gore; and Jamieson and

Waldman also indicate how framing of the debates aided the Bush camp (2003: 57ff).

[6] See the analysis of "Twenty-Five Bush Flubs in the Second Debate" and "Fifteen [Bush] Flubs in the Third Debate" at http://www.tompaine.com/ archives/index2.cfm?StartDate=%7Bts%20%272000%2D10%2D01%2000%3A 00%3A00%27%7D (February 20, 2004).

[7] A note on polls: The majority of the mainstream media polls on the eve of the election put Bush in the lead, sometimes as much as by 10 points during the final days of the election campaign (although the Zogby/Reuters and CBS News polls put Gore slightly ahead in the popular vote). Joan Didion reports, by contrast, that seven major academic pollsters presenting their data at the September 2000 American Political Science Association convention all predicted a big Gore victory, ranging from 60.3 percent to 52 percent of the vote. See Didion, "In God's Country," *The New York Review of Books* (November 2, 2000). Academic pollsters tend to use rational-choice models and base their results on economic indicators and in-depth interviews; they seem, however, to downplay moral values, issues of character, the role of media spectacle, and the fluctuating events of the election campaigns. Indeed, the academic pollsters argue that the electorate is basically fixed one or two months before the election. Arguably, however, US politics is more volatile and unpredictable and swayed by the contingencies of media spectacle, as Election 2000 and its aftermath dramatically demonstrate.

[8] A story in the *Washington Post* (February 9, 2001) by Robert G. Kaiser, "Experts Offer Mea Culpas for Predicting Gore Win," presents interviews with major political scientists who had predicted a strong win for Gore based on their mathematical models and data collected months before election day, seeing Gore winning from 52.8 to 60.3 percent of the national votes. One professor admitted that the "election outcome left a bit of egg on the faces of the academic forecasters," whereas others blamed a poor Gore campaign, "Clinton fatigue," and an unexpectedly strong showing by Ralph Nader. One defiant forecaster said that the election was simply weird, "on the fringe of our known world, a stochastic [random] shock."

[9] On political ads, see Milbank, 2001: 359ff and the study of television advertising by the Alliance for Better Campaigns, in Schechter, 2001: 77–92. In an illuminating study of ads in Election 2000, Lynda Lee Kaid argues that Bush's television ads established eye contact with viewers in 26 percent of his spots compared to only 6 percent for Gore. Bush was three times more likely to be shown with a smiling expression than Gore; and Bush was shown in close-up or tight shots in 41 percent of his ads compared to 24 percent for Gore, thus using video imagery to sell Bush's "personality" to voters. See "Videostyle and Technological Distortions in the 2000 Political

Spots," International Communications Association Convention, Washington, DC, May 2001.

[10] See MSNBC News, November 5 and November 15. For discussion of the *Saturday Night Live* effect, see Suck (November 16, 2000), and on comedy and the media, see Marshall Sella, "The Stiff Guy vs. the Dumb Guy," *New York Times* (September 24, 2000).

[11] See David Corn's analysis of how pundit predictions tended to call it decisively for Bush over Gore at http://www.tompaine.com/feature2.cfm/ID/3897 (February 20, 2004).

[12] See the following books on Bush's conservative but not compassionate record by Ivins and Dubose, 2000; Mitchell, 2000; Begala, 2000; Hatfield, 2000; and Miller, 2001.

[13] See Sussman, 1984 and Gabler, 1999: 197.

[14] For an excellent analysis of the qualifications of Gore to be president and lack of substantial achievements and qualifications of Bush, see Altermann, 2003: 148ff.

[15] Eric Altermann, "Al Gore, democrat," *The Nation*, October 21, 2002. Altermann repeats this analysis in 2003 and writes a whole chapter documenting mainstream media hatred toward Gore and complicity toward Bush (148–174). His book systematically devastates the myth of the "liberal media," savaging books that make this claim and providing extensive documentation of its nullity.

[16] On Bush's DWI incident and how his campaign and the Gore camp dealt with it, see Timothy J. Burger, "In the Driver's Seat: The Bush DUI," in Sabato, 2002: 69–93.

[17] For a good overview of the PEJ findings and critique of mainstream media news coverage of the election, see Bill Kovach and Tom Rosenstiel, "Campaign Lite: Why Reporters Won't Tell Us What We Need to Know," *Washington Monthly* (January/February 2001).

[18] For a wealth of studies of the media and politics of Election 2000 that document these claims, see the Project for Excellence in Journalism archived in http://www.journalism.org/ (February 20, 2004) and the studies in Schechter, 2001. In a *Columbia Journalism Review* article, "Gore Media Coverage—Playing Hardball," Jane Hall systematically analyzes negative and often misleading coverage of Gore, contrasted to soft and generally uncritical coverage of Bush (September/October 2000).

[19] For convincing demolitions of the allegation that Gore claimed to "invent" the Internet, see "The Red Herring Interview: E-Gore" (Red Herring, October 30, 2000).

[20] On Prescott Bush and Herbert Walker's management of National Socialist economic interests, see Tarpley and Chaitkin 1992: 26–44; Loftus and Aarons, 1994: 356–360; and Miller, 2001: 282.

[21] Doug Gamble cited in Martin A. Lee, <http://www.sfbg.com/reality/12.html>. See also, Miller's probing analysis (2001). *New York Times* correspondent Frank Bruni's history of Bush and the 2000 election (2002), by contrast, puts on display how Bush seduced the press and while Bruni complains about Bush's superficiality and the shallowness of political campaigns in the media age, his book exhibits the shallowness of the press and political correspondents.

[22] Archived in <http://www.cmpa.com (November 20, 2003). The Center for Media and Public Affairs (CMPA) is run by Robert Lichter, who has generally been perceived as a conservative critic of the media's liberal bias (although he claims to be a neutral social scientist), so it is interesting that his organization found a bias in favor of Bush. Later CMPA findings indicate that Gore's positive network news coverage went up sharply after the Democratic convention, as did Gore's ratings (September 5, 2000). But a study released by CMPA on October 18 indicated that "network news coverage of Al Gore turned sharply negative after the first presidential debate." It appears that CMPA's positive/negative network news codings of the candidates correlate remarkably with the candidates' rise and fall in the polls, although since polls themselves came under dramatic attack in the election, it is obviously not clear what exact impact positive and negative presentations of candidates on television news and in print have on voters. See also the discussion of positive/negative coding and the work of the German group Media Tenor in Markus Rettich, "Into the White House through the Television Screen," in Schechter, 2001: 100–102.

[23] See the summary in Schechter, 2001: 100f.

[24] A Lexis-Nexis search indicated that there were no references to the origins of the Bush family fortune in Union Banking Corporation that financed German National Socialism until an article by Michael Kranish, "Triumphs, Troubles shape generations," *Boston Globe* (April 23, 2001), including the following:

> Prescott Bush was surely aghast at a sensational article the New York Herald Tribune splashed on its front page in July 1942. "Hitler's Angel Has 3 Million in US Bank" read the headline above a story reporting that Adolf Hitler's financier had stowed the

fortune in Union Banking Corp, possibly to be held for "Nazi bigwigs."

Bush knew all about the New York bank: He was one of its seven directors. If the Nazi tie became known, it would be a potential "embarrassment," Bush and his partners at Brown Brothers Harriman worried, explaining to government regulators that their position was merely an unpaid courtesy for a client. The situation grew more serious when the government seized Union's assets under the Trading with the Enemy Act, the sort of action that could have ruined Bush's political dreams.

As it turned out, his involvement wasn't pursued by the press or political opponents during his Senate campaigns a decade later.

Although the Loftus and Aaron's study (1994) provided a well-documented exploration of connections between the bank that helped fund National Socialism and manage its US assets and businesses and the Bush dynasty, this episode was never explored by the US' corporate media. Neglect of the unsavory origins of the Bush family fortune and later financial scandals of the Bush family is one of the major journalistic and academic outrages in US history. Indeed, most books and articles on the Bushes are white-washes that repeat the same myths, and there has been little investigative study of the family by the media, political, and academic establishment. On other Bush family scandals and history, ignored by the mainstream media, see the material listed in Note 25 below.

[25] I cite books that document the scandals of Bush family history in notes 12 and 21, above, as well as in the text of this section. Web sites that document the history of Bush family scandals and George W. Bush's history include http://www.moldea.com (February 20, 2004); http://www.bushwatch.com (February 20, 2004); and http://prorev.com/bush3.htm (February 20, 2004). For a useful overview of Cheney's health, history, voting record, and hard-right credentials, see Begala 2000: 126–36.

[26] See the predictions compiled at http://www.tompaine.com/feature2.cfm/ID/3897 (February 20, 2004).

[27] See Jim Hightower's proposals for Electoral College reform at http://www.alternet.org/story.html?StoryID=10406 (February 20, 2004). In his December 4 online interview, Howard Kurtz noted that Gore would have won the Electoral College if every state received electoral votes in proportion to population: "Bush won 30 states for 271 and Gore won 21 for 267. But if you take away the two electors for each senator, and just apportion electors by number of Representatives (i.e., in proportion to population), Gore wins 225 to 211" http://www.washingtonpost.com/wp-srv/liveonline/00/politics/mediabacktalk120400.htm (February 20, 2004).

[28] In a chapter on "Electoral Reform" after Election 2000, Ceaser and Busch lay out the case for proportional presentation system, opposed to a direct popular majority vote electoral system, but do not consider the strong arguments that I cite above to eliminate the "unfaithful elector" problem by mandating direct presidential voting, nor do they take seriously arguments against the current US system of proportional voting. In any case, in the current political climate there is little pressure for major electoral reform, although on the local level there have been attempts to require updating of voting machines, streamlining of voting processes, stipulation of recount procedures, and other technical changes to avoid the debacle of the Florida nightmare.

[29] On the history of efforts to reform television advertising, see Charles Lewis, "You Get What You Pay For: How Corporate Spending Blocked Political Ad Reform & Other Stories of Influence" (Schechter, 2001: 62–73) and the Alliance for Better Campaigns, "Gouging Democracy: How the Television Industry Profiteered on Campaign 2000," in Schechter ,2001 (77–92). In another important article in Schechter (2001: 75), Lawrence K. Grossman notes that one of broadcasting's "dirty little secrets" is its "sustained and high-priced lobbying against finance reform."

References

Aden, R. C. 1989. Televised Political Advertising: A Review of Literature on Spots. *Political Communication* 14:1. pp. 1–18.

Aguilera de Prat, C. 1999. *El Cambio Politico en Italia y la Liga Norte.* Madrid: CIS.

Allensbacher Archiv. August 1998. *IfD–Umfrage 6063.* Allensbach: Institut für Demoskopie.

Altermann, E. 2000. *Sound and Fury: The Making of the Punditocracy.* Ithaca, NY: Cornell University Press.

Ansolabehere, S., and Iyengar, S. 1995. *Going Negative: How Attack Ads Shrink and Polarize the Electorate.* New York: The Free Press.

Anti-MMP. 6 July 1993. Anti-MMP appeal. *New Zealand Herald.* p. 3.

———. 2003. *What Liberal Media? The Truth about Bias and the News.* New York: Basic Books.

Bartolini S., and R. D'Alimonte, Eds. 2002. *Maggioritario Finalmente? La Transizione Elettorale 1994–2001.* Bologna: Il Mulino.

———., and R. D'Alimonte. 1995. La Competizione Maggioritaria: Le Origini Elettorali del Parlamento Diviso. In S. Bartolini and R. D'Alimonte, Eds. *Maggioritario ma non Troppo.* pp. 317–372. Bologna: Il Mulino.

———., and R. D'Alimonte. 2002. Premessa. In S. Bartolini and R. D'Alimonte, Eds. *Maggioritario Finalmente? La Transizione Elettorale 1994–2001.* pp. 7–15. Bologna: Il Mulino.

———., and R. D'Alimonte. 2002. La Maggioranza Ritrovata. La Competizione nei Collegi Uninominali. In S. Bartolini and R. D'Alimonte, Eds. 2002. *Maggioritario Finalmente? La Transizione Elettorale 1994–2001.* pp. 199–248. Bologna: Il Mulino.

Begala, P. 2000. *Is Our Children Learning? The Case Against George W. Bush.* New York: Simon and Schuster.

Bertram, G. 1997. Macroeconomic debate and economic growth in postwar New Zealand. In B. Roper and C. Rudd, Eds. *The political economy of New Zealand.* pp. 40–59. Auckland: Oxford University Press.

Birch, A. 1993. *The Concepts and Theories of Modern Democracy.* London and New York: Routledge.

Blumler, J., and M. Gurevitch. 1995. *The Crisis of Public Communication*. London: Routledge.

Booker, M. 24 June 1993. MMP move fires up opposing factions. *The Dominion*. p. 21.

Bourdieu, P. 1991. *Language and Symbolic Power*. Trans. G. Raymond and M. Adamson. Cambridge, MA: Harvard University Press.

Brewton, P. 1992. *The Mafia, CIA and George Bush*. New York: SPI Books.

Bruni, F. 2002. *Ambling Into History*. New York: HarperCollins.

Buß, M., M. Darkow, R. Ehlers, H.-J. Weiß, and K. Zimmer. 1984. *Fernsehen und Alltag. Eine ARD/ZDF–Studie im Wahljahr 1980*. Frankfurt am Main: Alfred Metzner.

Bugiliosi, V. 2001. *The Betrayal of America: How the Supreme Court Undermined the Constitution and Chose Our President*. New York: Thunder's Mouth Press/Nation Books.

Calise, M. 2000. *Il Partito Personale*. Rome: Laterza.

Caspari, M., K. Schönbach, and E. Lauf. May 1999. Bewertung politischer Akteure in Fernsehnachrichten. *Media Perspektiven*. pp. 270–274.

Ceaser, J., and Andrew E. Busch. 2001. *The Perfect Tie*. Lanham, MD: Rowman and Littlefield.

Cheles, L. 2001. Picture Battles in the Piazza: The Political Poster. In L. Cheles and L. Sponza, Eds. *The Art of Persuasion: Political Communication in Italy from 1945 to the 1990s*. pp. 124–179. Manchester: Manchester University Press.

Clifton, J. 6 October 1996. Fuming Lange Snubs Clark. *Sunday Star Times*. p. 1.

Cotta, M. 2002. Dopo Tre Elezioni: Il Sistema Politico Italiano a Dieci Anni Dalla Crisi. In S. Bartolini and R. D'Alimonte, Eds. *Maggioritario Finalmente? La Transizione Elettorale 1994–2001*. pp. 17–40. Bologna: Il Mulino.

Cowen, P. B., Cowen, T., and Tabbarok, A. (1992). *An Analysis of Proposals for Constitutional Change in New Zealand*. Wellington: New Zealand Business Roundtable.

Cox, G. W. 1997. *Making Votes Count. Strategic Coordination in the World's Electoral Systems*. Cambridge: Cambridge University Press.

D'Alimonte, R., and A. Chiaramonte. 1995. Il Nuovo Sistema Elettorale Italiano: Le Opportunitá e le Scelte. In S. Bartolini and

R. D'Alimonte, Eds. *Maggioritario ma non Troppo.* pp. 37–81. Bologna: Il Mulino.

Dahlgren, P. 1995. *Television and the Public Sphere.* London: Sage.

Dershowitz, A. 2001. Supreme Injustice: *How the High Court Hijacked Election 2000.* New York: Oxford University Press.

Diamond, E., and S. Bates. 1992. *The Spot: The Rise of Political Advertising on Television,* 3rd ed. Cambridge, MA: MIT Press.

Di Virgilio, A. 1997. Le Alleanze Elettorali: Identitá Partitiche e Logiche Coalizionali. In S. Bartolini and R. D'Alimonte, Eds. 1997. *Maggioritario per Caso: Le Elezioni Politiche del 1996.* pp. 71–135. Bologna: Il Mulino.

―――. 1998. Electoral Alliances: Party Identities and Coalition Games. *European Journal of Political Research* 34. pp. 5–33.

―――. 2002. L'offerta Elettorale: La Politica Delle Alleanze Si Istituzionalizza. In S. Bartolini and R. D'Alimonte, Eds. *Maggioritario Finalmente? La Transizione Elettorale 1994–2001.* pp. 79–129. Bologna: Il Mulino.

Donovan, M. 1995. The Politics of Electoral Reform in Italy. *International Political Science Review* 16. pp. 47–64.

Duverger, M. 1951. *Les Partis Politiques.* Paris: Colin.

―――. 1963. *Political Parties. Their Organization and Activity in the Modern State.* New York: Wiley.

Falter, J. W. 1981. Kontinuität und Neubeginn. Die Bundestagswahl 1949 zwischen Weimar und Bonn. *Politische Vierteljahresschrift* 22. pp. 236–263.

Fisher, S. L. 1973. The Wasted Vote Thesis: West German Evidence. *Comparative Politics* 5. pp. 293–299.

Franklin, B. 1994. *Packaging Politics.* London: Edward Arnold.

Fusaro, C. 1995. *Le Regole della Transizione.* Bologna: Il Mulino.

Gabler, Neil 1998. *Life the Movie: How Entertainment Conquered Reality.* New York: Alfred A. Knopf.

Geiger, S. F., and B. Reeves. 1991. The Effects of Visual Structure and Content Emphasis on the Evaluation and Memory for Political Candidates. In F. Biocca, Ed. 1991. *Television and Political Advertising. Volume 1: Psychological Processes.* pp. 125–143. Hillsdale, NJ: Lawrence Erlbaum.

Gitlin, T. 1991. Bites and Blips: Chunk News, Savvy Talk and the Bifurcation of American Politics. In P. Dahlgren and C. Sparks, Eds. *Communication and Citizenship: Journalism and the Public Sphere.* pp. 119–136. London: Routledge.

Görtemaker, M. 1999. *Geschichte der Bundesrepublik Deutschland. Von der Gründung bis zur Gegenwart.* Munich: C. H. Beck.

Greenfield, J. 1982. *The Real Campaign: How the Media Missed the Story of the 1980 Campaign.* New York: Summit Books.

Greenfield, J. 2001. *Oh Wait! One Order of Crow: Inside the Strangest Presidential Election Finish in American History.* New York: Putnam.

Habermas, J. 1991. *The structural transformation of the public sphere* (Thomas Burger, Trans.). Cambridge, Mass: MIT Press.

Haeusler, J., and Hirsch, J. 1989. Political Regulation: The Crisis of Fordism and the Transformation of the Party System in West Germany. In M. Gottdiener & A. Kominos (Eds.), *Capitalist Development and Crisis Theory: Accumulation, Regulation and Spatial Restructuring.* pp. 300-327. New York: St Martin's Press.

Hall, S. 1986. On Postmodernism and Articulation. *Journal of Communication Inquiry* 10:2. pp. 45–60.

Hatfield, J. H. 2000. *Fortunate Son: George W. Bush and the Making of an American President.* New York: Soft Skull Press.

Herman, E., and N. Chomsky. 1988. *Manufacturing Consent: The Political Economy of the Mass Media.* New York: Pantheon.

Hilmer, R., and N. Schleyer. 2000. Stimmensplitting bei der Bundestagswahl 1998. Strukturen, Trends und Motive. In J. van Deth, H. Rattinger and E. Roller, Eds. *Die Republik auf dem Weg zur Normalität? Wahlverhalten und politische Einstellungen nach acht Jahren Einheit.* pp. 173–197. Opladen: Leske+Budrich.

Holtz-Bacha, C., and Kaid, L. L. 1995. A Comparative Perspective on Political Advertising: Media and Political System Characteristics. In C. Holtz-Bacha and L. L. Kaid, Eds. *Political advertising in Western democracies: Parties and candidates on television.* pp. 8-18. Thousand Oaks: Sage Publications Inc.

Holtz–Bacha, C. 2002. Professionalization of Political Communication. The Case of the 1998 SPD Campaign. *Journal of Political Marketing* 1. pp. 23–37.

———. 2000. *Wahlwerbung als politische Kultur. Parteienspots im Fernsehen 1957–1998.* Wiesbaden: Westdeutscher Verlag.

———., and L. L. Kaid. 1996. Simply the best. Parteienspots im Bundestags wahlkampf 1994 — Inhalte und Rezeption. In C. Holtz–Bacha and L. L. Kaid, Eds. *Wahlen und Wahlkampf in den Medien. Untersuchungen aus Dem Wahljahr 1994.* pp. 177–207. Opladen: Westdeutscher Verlag.

————., E. M. Lessinger, and M. Hettesheimer. 1998. Personalisierung als Strategie der Wahlwerbung. In K. Imhof and P. Schulz, Eds. *Die Veröffentlichung des Privaten—die Privatisierung des Öffentlichen.* pp. 240–250. Opladen: Westdeutscher Verlag.

Hubbard, A. 6 July 1997. Perfectly Good System, but Badly Run. *Sunday Star Times.* p. C2.

Ignazi, P. 1995. Italy. *European Journal of Political Research* 28. pp. 393–405.

Ivins, M., and L. Dubose 2000. *Shrub: The Short but Happy Political Life of George W. Bush.* New York: Random House.

Jackson, W. K. 1993. The Origins of the Electoral Referendums. In McRobie, Ed. *Taking it to the people.* pp. 15–23. Christchurch: Hazard Press.

Jamieson, K. H. 1992. *Dirty Politics.* New York: Oxford University Press.

Jamieson, K. H., and P. Waldman. 2003. *The Press Effect.* New York: Oxford University Press.

Jesse, E. 1997. Die Parteien im westlichen Deutschland von 1945 bis zur Deutschen Einheit 1990. In O. W. Gabriel, O. Niedermayer and R. Stöss, Eds. *Parteiendemokratie in Deutschland.* pp. 59–83. Opladen: Westdeutscher Verlag.

————. 1988. Split–voting in the Federal Republic of Germany: An analysis of the federal elections from 1953 to 1987. *Electoral Studies* 7. pp. 109–124.

————. 2001. Ist das Wahlsystem zum Deutschen Bundestag reformbedürftig? Eine politikwissenschaftliche Analyse. In H–D. Klingemann and M. Kaase, Eds. *Wahlen und Wähler. Analysen aus Anlass der Bundestagswahl 1998.* pp. 503–527. Wiesbaden: Westdeutscher Verlag.

Johnson–Cartee, K. S., and G. A. Copeland. 1991. *Negative Political Advertising: Coming of Age.* Hillsdale, NJ: Lawrence Erlbaum Associates, Inc.

Jones, N. 1995. *Soundbites and Spin Doctors: How Politicians Manipulate the Media and Vice Versa.* London: Cassell.

Kaid, L. L., and K. R. Sanders. 1978. Political Television Commercials: An Experimental Study of Type and Length. *Communication Research* 5. pp. 57–70.

Katz, R. 1995. The 1993 Parliamentary Electoral Reform. In C. Mershon and G. Pasquino, Eds. 1993. *Italian Politics: Ending the First Republic.* pp. 93–112. Boulder, CO: Westview Press.

Kavanagh, D. 1995. *Election Campaigning: The New Marketing of Politics.* Oxford: Blackwell.

van Kempen, H. July 2002. *Mobilizing Electorates. A Study of Mobilizing Communication Forces in the European Elections of 1999.* Paper presented at the ICA conference, Seoul, Korea.

Kellner, D. 1990. *Television and the Crisis of Democracy.* Boulder, CO: Westview Press.

Kelsey, J. 1997. *The New Zealand Experiment: A World Model for Structural Adjustment?* 2nd ed. Auckland: Auckland University Press.

———. 1992. *The Persian Gulf TV War.* Boulder, CO: Westview Press.

———. 2001. *Grand Theft 2000.* Lanham, MD: Rowman and Littlefield.

Kern, M. 1989. *30–Second Politics.* New York: Praeger Publishers.

Kirk, J. 8 April 1996. Alliance to Go Back to Basics. *The Press.* p. 3.

Kirchheimer, O. 1966. The Transformation of the Western European Party Systems. In J. La Palombara and M. Weiner, Eds. *Political Parties and Political Development.* pp. 177–200. Princeton: Princeton University Press.

Klingemann, H.D. 1970. *Bestimmungsgründe der Wahlentscheidung.* Meisenheim am Glan: Anton Hain.

Knoche, M., and M. Lindgens. 1990. Fünf–Prozent–Hürde und Medienbarriere. Die Grünen im Bundestagswahlkampf 1987: Neue Politik, Medienpräsenz und Resonanz in der Wählerschaft. In M. Kaase and H–D. Klingemann, Eds. *Wahlen und Wähler. Analysen aus Anlaß der Bundestagswahl 1987.* pp. 569–618. Opladen: Westdeutscher Verlag.

Kovach, B., and Rosenstiel, T. Jan–Feb 2001. Campaign Lite: Why Reporters Won't Tell Us What We Need to Know. *Washington Monthly.*

Lange, D. 24 June 1996. Hamming it up on Overseas Junkets. *Waikato Times.* p. 6.

Lange, E. H. M. 1975. *Wahlrecht und Innenpolitik. Entstehungsgeschichte und Analyse der Wahlgesetzgebung und Wahlrechtsdiskussion im westlichen Nachkriegsdeutschland 1945–1956.* Meisenheim am Glan: Anton Hain.

Langenbucher, W. R. 1983. Wahlkampf ein ungeliebtes, notwendiges Übel? In W. Schulz and K. Schönbach, Eds. *Massenmedien und Wahlen. Mass Media and Elections: International Research Perspectives.* pp. 114–128. Munich: Ölschläger.

Langenbucher, W. R., and H. R. Uekermann. 1985. Politische Kommunikationsrituale. In F. Plasser, P. A. Ulram and M. Welan, Eds. *Demokratierituale. Zur Politischen Kultur der Informationsgesellschaft.* pp. 49–59. Wien: Hermann Böhlaus Nachf.

Laugesen, R. 24 October 1999. Clark in Bed with Greenies. *Sunday Star Times.* pp. A1–2.

Lemert, J., et al. 1996. *The Politics of Disenchantment.* Cresskill, NJ: Hampton.

Levine, S., and Roberts, N. S. 1993. The New Zealand Electoral Referendum of 1993. *Electoral Studies* 12. pp. 158–167.

Levine, M. 1995. *Presidential Campaigns and Elections: Issues and Images in the Media Age,* 2nd ed. Itasca, IL: F.E. Peacock.

Lijphart, A. 1999. *Patterns of Democracy. Government Forms and Performance in Thirty–Six Countries.* New Haven: Yale University Press.

Loftus, J., and Aarons, M. 1994. *The Secret War Against the Jews.* New York: St Martin's Press.

Maarek, P. 1995. *Political Marketing and Communication.* London: John Libbey.

Mackie, T. 2000. Quotas and Divisors. In R. Rose, Ed. *International Encyclopedia of Elections.* pp. 252–253. London: Macmillan.

McCarten, M. 2000. The Alliance Election Strategy. In J. Boston, et al., Eds. *Left Turn: The New Zealand General Election of 1999.* pp. 36–40. Wellington: Victoria University Press.

McManus, J. 9 July 1993. Anti-MMP Ads Prey on Public Anxiety. *The Independent.* pp. 1,2, 4.

Main, V. 25 October 1995. Public Set to Muddle MMP Votes Says Poll. *The Dominion.* p. 1.

Mancini, P., and G. Mazzoleni, Eds. 1995. *I Media Scendono in Campo. La Campagna Elettorale del 1994.* Rome: ERI/Vqpt.

———., and D. Swanson. 1996. Politics, Media, and Modern Democracy: Introduction. In D. Swanson and P. Mancini, Eds. *Politics, Media, and Modern Democracy.* pp. 1–26. Westport, CT: Praeger.

Marini, R., and F. Roncarolo. 1997. *I Media come Arena Elettorale. Le Elezioni Politiche 1966 in TV e nei Giornali.* Rome: ERI/Vqpt.

Mayhew, L. 1997. *The New Public: Professional Communication and the Means of Social Influence.* Cambridge: Cambridge University Press.

Mazzoleni, G. 1987. The Role of Private Television Stations in Italian Elections. In D. Paletz, Ed. *Political Communication Research.* pp. 75–87. Norwood, NJ: Ablex.

———. 1991. Emergence of the Candidate and Political Marketing: Television and Election Campaigns in Italy in the 1980s. *Political Communication and Persuasion* 8. pp. 201–212.

———. 1995. Towards a Videocracy? Italian Political Communication at a Turning Point. *European Journal of Communication* 10. pp. 291–319.

———. 1996. Patterns and Effects of Recent Changes in Electoral Campaigning in Italy. In D. Swanson and P. Mancini, Eds. *Politics, Media, and Modern Democracy.* pp. 193–206. Westport, CT: Praeger.

———., and W. Schulz. 1999. Mediatization of Politics: A Challenge for Democracy? *Political Communication* 16. pp. 247–261.

Melchionda, E. 2002. L'alternanza Prevista. La Competizione nei Collegi Uninominali. In G. Pasquino, Ed. *Dall'Ulivo al Governo Berlusconi. Le Elezioni del 13 Maggio 2001 e il Sistema Politico Italiano.* pp. 23–105. Bologna: Il Mulino.

Michie, D. 1998. *The Invisible Persuaders.* London: Bantam Press.

Milbank, D. 2001. *Smashmouth: Two Years in the Gutter with Al Gore and George W. Bush .* New York: Basic Books.

Miller, R., and Catt, H. 1993. *Season of Discontent.* Palmerston North: Dunmore Press.

Miller, R. 1998. Coalition Government: The People's Choice? In J. Vowles, P. Aimer, S. Banducci, and J. Karp, Eds. *Voters' victory? New Zealand's first election under proportional representation.* pp. 120–134. Auckland: Auckland University Press.

Miller, M. C. 2001. *The Bush Dyslexicon.* New York: Norton.

Mitchell, E. 2000. *Revenge of the Bush Dynasty.* New York: Hyperion.

Mold, F., and J. Armstrong. 22 July 2002. Worm Debate Makes Dunne Powerbroker. *The New Zealand Herald.* p. A1.

Moffitt, M. A. 1994. Collapsing and Integrating Concepts of "Public" and "Image" into a New Theory. *Public Relations Review*, 20. pp. 159–170.

Morlino, L. 1997. Is There an Impact? And Where is It? Electoral Reform and the Party System in Italy. *South European Society and Politics* 2. pp. 103–130.

Mouffe, C. 1993. *The Return of the Political*. London: Verso.

Mudambi, R., P. Navarra, and G. Sobbrio. 2001. *Rules, Choice and Strategy: The Political Economy of Italian Electoral Reform*. Cheltenham: Edward Elgar.

Nadel, M. 1976. *Corporations and Political Accountability*. Lexington, Mass: D.C. Heath and Company.

Natale, P. 2002. Una Fedeltà Leggera: I Movimenti di Voto Nella 'Seconda Repubblica'. In S. Bartolini and R. D'Alimonte, Eds. *Maggioritario Finalmente? La Transizione Elettorale 1994–2001*. pp. 283–317. Bologna: Il Mulino.

Newman, B. 1994. *The Marketing of the President: Political Marketing as Campaign Strategy*. London: Sage.

Nichols, J. 2001. *Jews for Buchanan*. New York: The New Press.

Niedermayer, O. 1997. Das gesamtdeutsche Parteiensystem. In O. W. Gabriel, O. Niedermayer and R. Stöss, Eds. *Parteiendemokratie in Deutschland*. pp.106–130. Opladen: Westdeutscher Verlag.

Nimmo, D. 1996. Politics, Media, and Modern Democracy: The United States. In D. Swanson and P. Mancini, Eds. *Politics, Media, and Modern Democracy*. pp. 29–47. Westport, CT: Praeger.

Nohlen, D. 2000. *Wahlrecht und Parteiensystem*. 3rd ed. Opladen: Leske+Budrich.

————., et al. 2000. Electoral Systems in Independent Countries. In R. Rose, Ed. *International Encyclopedia of Elections*. pp. 353–379 (Appendix). London: Macmillan.

Norris, P. 1995. Introduction: The Politics of Electoral Reforms. *International Political Science Review* 16. pp. 3–8.

Oliver, P. 29–30 June 2002. Lessons in Camouflage for Political Donors. *Weekend Herald* . p. B3.

O'Sullivan, F., and Small, V. 29–30 June 2002. Labour Courts Anonymous Business Cash. *Weekend Herald*. p. A1.

Palmer, G. 1987. *Unbridled Power: An Interpretation of New Zealand's Constitution and Government*, 2nd ed. Auckland: Oxford University Press.

Parisi, A. 1980. *Mobilità Senza Movimento*. Bologna: Il Mulino.

————., and G. Pasquino. 1977. Relazioni Partiti–Elettori e Tipi di Voto. In A. Parisi and G. Pasquino, Eds. *Continuità e Mutamento elettorale in Italia*. pp. 215–250. Bologna: Il Mulino.

Parry, R. 1992. *Fooling America: How Washington Insiders Twist the Truth and Manufacture the Conventional Wisdom*. New York: Morrow.

————., and H.M.A. Schadee, Eds. 1995. *Sulla Soglia del Cambiamento. Elettori e Partiti alla Fine della Prima Repubblica*. Bologna: Il Mulino.

Pasquino, G., Ed. 2002. *Dall'Ulivo al Governo Berlusconi. Le Elezioni del 13 Maggio 2001 e il Sistema Politico Italiano*. pp. 23–105. Bologna: Il Mulino.

————. 2002. *Il Sistema Politico Italiano*. Bologna: Bononia University Press.

Pezzini, I. 2001. Advertising Politics on Television: The Party Election Broadcast. In L. Cheles and L. Sponza, Eds. *The Art of Persuasion. Political Communication in Italy from 1945 to the 1990s*. pp. 180–195. Manchester: Manchester University Press.

Powell, G. B., Jr. 2000. *Elections as Instruments of Democracy Majoritarian and Proportional Visions*. New Haven: Yale University Press.

Recker, M–L. 1997. Wahlen und Wahlkämpfe in der Bundesrepublik Deutschland 1949–1969. In G. A. Ritter, Ed. *Wahlen und Wahlkämpfe in Deutschland. Von den Anfängen im 19. Jahrhundert bis zur Bundesrepublik*. pp. 267–309. Düsseldorf: Droste.

Reumann, K. 9 March 1983. Gib es Einen Fallbeil–Effekt für die kleinen Parteien? *Frankfurter Allgemeine Zeitung*. p. 4.

Riker, W. 1982. The Two–party System and Duverger's Law: An Essay on the History of Political Science. *American Political Science Review* 76. pp. 753–766.

Roberts, G. K. 1988. The "Second–Vote" Campaign Strategy of the West German Free Democratic Party. *European Journal of Political Research* 16. pp. 317–337.

Roper, J., and Leitch, S. 1995. The Electoral Reform Campaigns in New Zealand: A Political Communication Case Study. *Australian Journal of Communication*, 22. pp. 123–135.

Roper, J. 1999. The Turn of the Worm: The Framing of Press and Television Coverage of Televised Election Debates in New Zealand. *Australian Journal of Communication* 26:1. pp. 1–20.

Rosenbaum, M. 1997. *From Soapbox to Soundbite: Party Political Campaigning in Britain since 1945.* Basingstoke: Macmillan.

Rudd, R. 1986. Issues as Image in Political Campaign Commercials. *Western Journal of Speech Communication* 50. pp. 102–118.

Sabato, L. A., Ed. 2002. *Overtime! The Election 2000 Thriller.* New York: Longman.

Sartori, G. 2002. Il Sistema Elettorale Resta Cattivo. In G. Pasquino, Ed. *Dall'Ulivo al Governo Berlusconi. Le Elezioni del 13 Maggio 2001 e il Sistema Politico Italiano.* pp. 107–115. Bologna: Il Mulino.

Scammell, M. 1995. *Designer Politics: How Elections are Won.* Basingstoke: Macmillan.

Scammell, M., and H. Semetko. 1995. Political Advertising on Television: The British Experience. In C. Holtz–Bacha and L. L. Kaid, Eds. *Political Advertising in Western Democracies: Parties and Candidates on Television.* pp. 19–43. Thousand Oaks, CA: Sage.

Schechter, D. 2001. *Mediocracy 2000 Hail to the Thief: How the Media Stole the U.S. Presidential Election.* Electronic book available through http://www.newsdissector.org/dissectorville (March 28, 2004).

Semetko, H., Blumler, J. G., Gurevitch, M., and Weaver, D. H. 1991. *The Formation of Campaign Agendas: A Comparative Analysis of Party and Media Roles in Recent American and British Elections.* New Jersey: Lawrence Erlbaum Associates.

Shea, D. 1996. *Campaign Craft.* Westport, CT: Praeger.

Schmitt–Beck, R. 1993. Denn sie wissen nicht, was sie tun . . . Zum Verständnis des Verfahrens der Bundestagswahl bei westdeutschen und ostdeutschen Wählern. *Zeitschrift für Parlamentsfragen* 24. pp. 393–415.

———. 1996. Medien und Mehrheiten: Massenmedien als Informationsvermittler über die Wahlchancen der Parteien. *Zeitschrift für Parlamentsfragen* 27. pp. 393–415.

Schneider, M., K. Schönbach., and H. Semetko. May 1999. Kanzlerkandidaten in den Fernsehnachrichten und in der Wählermeinung. *Media Perspektiven.* pp. 262–269.

Schoen, H. 1998. Stimmensplitting bei Bundestagswahlen: eine Form taktischer Wahlentscheidung? *Zeitschrift für Parlamentsfragen* 29. pp. 223–244.

———. 2000. Eine oder zwei Stimmen. Fundierte Debatte oder viel Lärm um nichts? In J. van Deth, H. Rattinger, and E. Roller, Eds.

Die Republik auf dem Weg zur Normalität? Wahlverhalten und Politische Einstellungen nach acht Jahren Einheit. pp. 145–172. Opladen: Leske+Budrich.

————. 2000. Appelle zu taktischem Wahlverhalten. Effektive Werbung oder verfehlte Wahlkampfrhetorik? In J. Falter, O. W. Gabriel and H. Rattinger, Eds. *Wirklich ein Volk? Die politischen Orientierungen von Ost–und Westdeutschen im Vergleich.* pp. 643–673. Opladen: Leske+Budrich.

Schrott, P. 1990. Wahlkampfdebatten im Fernsehen 1972 bis 1987: Politikerstrategien und Wählerreaktion. In M. Kaase and H–D. Klingemann, Eds. *Wahlen und Wähler. Analysen aus Anlaß der Bundestagswahl 1987.* pp. 647–674. Opladen: Westdeutscher Verlag.

Semetko, H. A., and K. Schoenbach. 1994. *Germany's "Unity Election": Voters and the Media.* Cresskill, NJ: Hampton.

Shugart, M., and Wattenburg, M, Eds. (2001). *Mixed–member Electoral Systems: The Best of Both Worlds.* Oxford: Oxford University Press.

Simon, R. (2001). *Divided We Stand. How Al Gore Beat George Bush and Lost the Presidency.* New York: Crown Publishers.

Slack, J. 1996. The Theory and Method of Articulation in Cultural Studies. In D. Morley and K. H. Chen, Eds. *Stuart Hall: Critical Dialogues in Cultural Studies.* pp. 112–127. London: Routledge.

Smellie, P. 7 November 1999. Voters Warm to MMP. *Sunday Star Times.* p. A2.

Statera, G. 1986. *La Politica Spettacolo. Politici e Mass Media nell'Era dell'Immagine.* Milan: Mondadori.

Sussman, W. 1984. *Culture as History: The Transformation of American Society in the Twentieth Century.* New York: Pantheon.

Swanson, D., and P. Mancini, Eds. 1996. *Politics, Media and Modern Democracy.* Westport, CT: Praeger.

————., and P. Mancini. 1996. Patterns of Modern Electoral Campaigning and their Consequences. In D. Swanson and P. Mancini, Eds. *Politics, Media and Modern Democracy.* pp. 247–276. Westport, CT: Praeger.

Tapper, J. 2001. *Down and Dirty: The Plot to Steal the Presidency.* Boston: Little, Brown.

Tarpley, W. G., and A. Chaitkin. 1992. *George Bush. The Unauthorized Biography.* Washington, DC: Executive Intelligence Review.

Thurner, P. 1999. Taktisch Oder Aufrichtig? Zur Untersuchung des Stimmensplittings bei Bundestagswahlen. *Zeitschrift für Parlamentsfragen* 30. pp. 163–165.

Toman–Banke, M. 1996. *Die Wahlslogans der Bundestagswahlen 1949–1994*. Wiesbaden: DeutscherUniversitätsVerlag.

Toobin, J. 2001. *Too Close to Call*. New York: Random House.

Vassallo, S. 1997. Struttura della Competizione e Risultato Elettorale. In P. Corbetta and A. Parisi. *A Domanda Risponde*. pp. 21–79. Bologna: Il Mulino.

Venter, N. 30 October 1999. Nats Face Friendly Fire as ACT Comes Out Fighting. *The Dominion*. p. 2.

Vowles, J., and Aimer, P. 1993. *Voters' Vengeance*. Auckland: Auckland University Press.

Vowles, J. 1995. The Politics of Electoral Reform in New Zealand. *International Political Science Review* 16. pp. 95-115.

Vowles, J., Aimer, P., Catt, H., Lamare, J., and Miller, R. (1995). *Towards consensus? The 1993 General Election in New Zealand and the Transition to Proportional Representation*. Auckland: Auckland University Press.

Vowles, J. 1998. Countdown to MMP. In J. Vowles, P. Aimer, S. Banducci, and J. Karp, Eds. *Voters' Victory? New Zealand's FirstEelection Under Proportional Representation*. pp. 12-27. Auckland: Auckland University Press.

Vowles, J., Aimer, P., Banducci, S., and Karp, J. 1998. Expectations of Change. In J. Vowles, P. Aimer, S. Banducci, and J. Karp, Eds. *Voters' Victory? New Zealand's First Election Under Proportional Representation*. Auckland: Auckland University Press.

Wernick, A. 1991. *Promotional Culture. Advertising, Ideology and Symbolic Expression*. London: Sage.

Young, A. 2000. Strategy, Tactics, and Operations: National's Campaign. In J. Boston, et al., Eds. *Left Turn: The New Zealand General Election of 1999*. pp. 30–35. Wellington: Victoria University Press.

———. 3–4 August 2002. Into the Valley of Death. *Weekend Herald*. pp. B1 and B3.

POLITICAL COMMUNICATION

FRONTIERS IN

General Editors
Lynda Lee Kaid and Bruce Gronbeck

At the heart of how citizens, governments, and the media interact is the communication process, a process that is undergoing tremendous changes as we embrace a new millennium. Never has there been a time when confronting the complexity of these evolving relationships been so important to the maintenance of civil society. This series seeks books that advance the understanding of this process from multiple perspectives and as it occurs in both institutionalized and non-institutionalized political settings. While works that provide new perspectives on traditional political communication questions are welcome, the series also encourages the submission of manuscripts that take an innovative approach to political communication, which seek to broaden the frontiers of study to incorporate critical and cultural dimensions of study as well as scientific and theoretical frontiers.

For more information or to submit material for consideration, contact:

BRUCE E. GRONBECK
Obermann Center for Advanced Studies
N134 OH
The University of Iowa
Iowa City, IA 52242-5000

LYNDA LEE KAID
Political Communication Center
Department of Communication
University of Oklahoma
Norman, OK 73109

To order other books in this series, please contact our Customer Service Department:

(800) 770-LANG (within the U.S.)
(212) 647-7706 (outside the U.S.)
(212) 647-7707 FAX

Or browse online by series:
WWW.PETERLANGUSA.COM